This Book Belongs to

© 2018 All rights Reserved

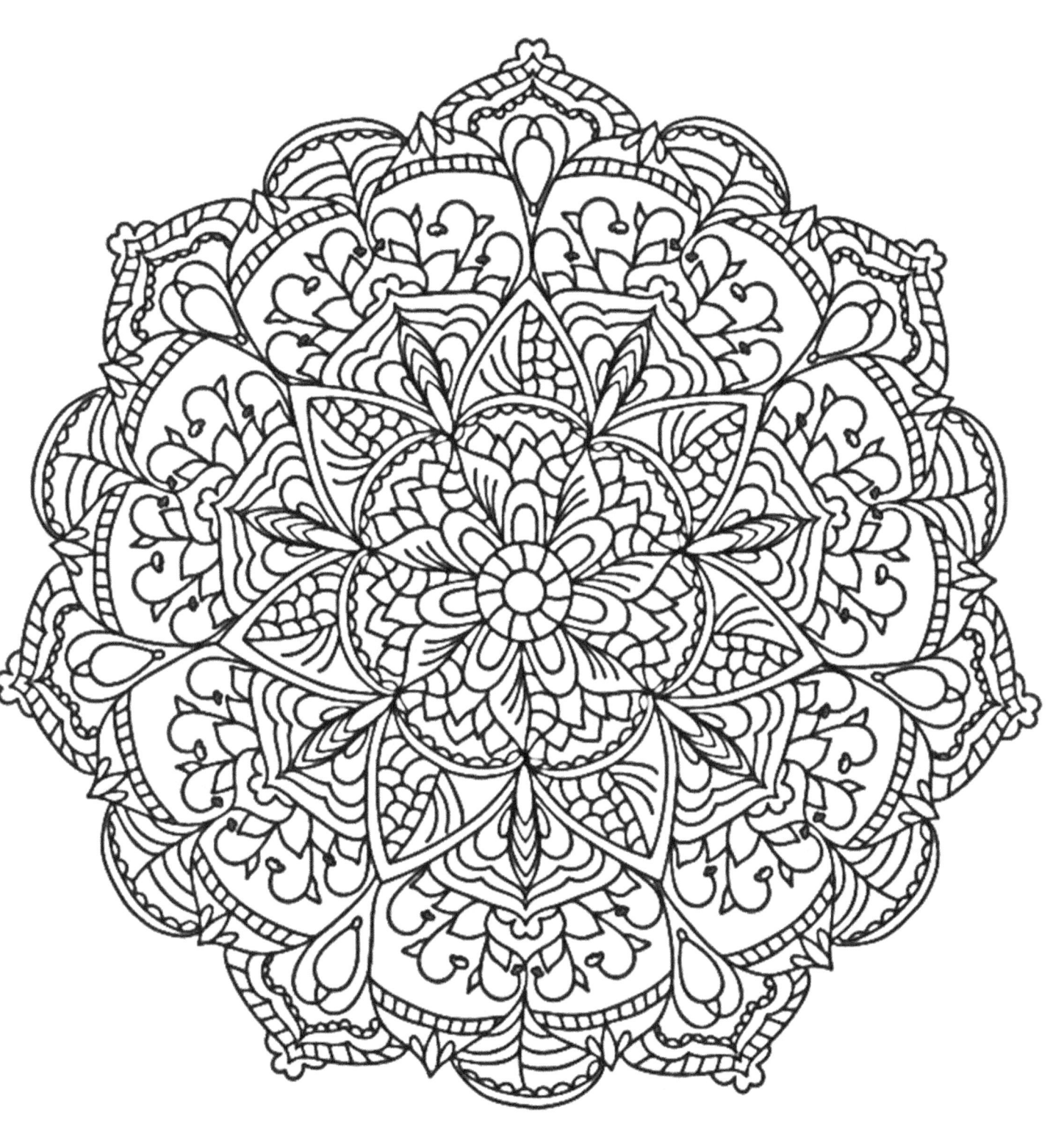

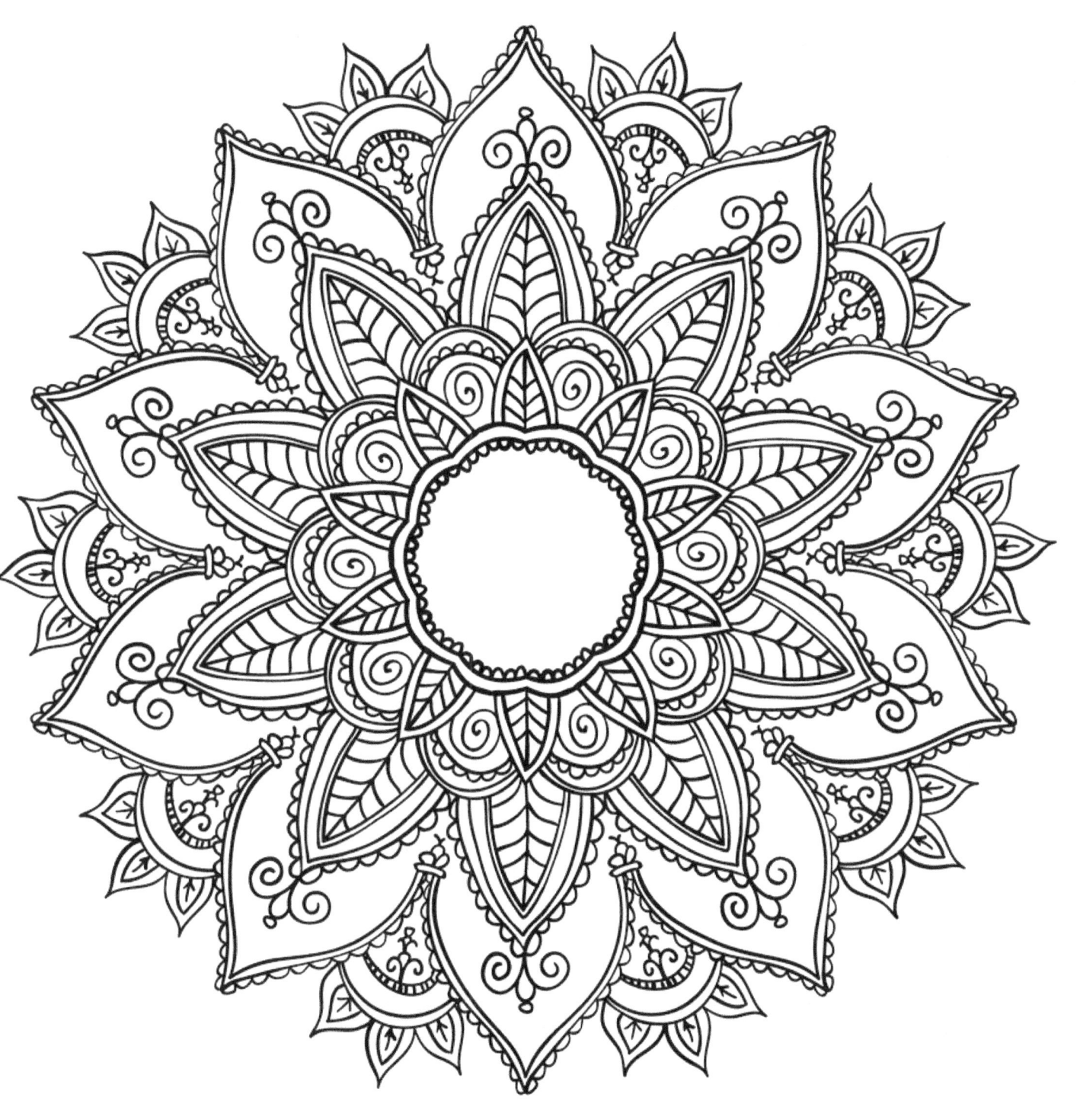

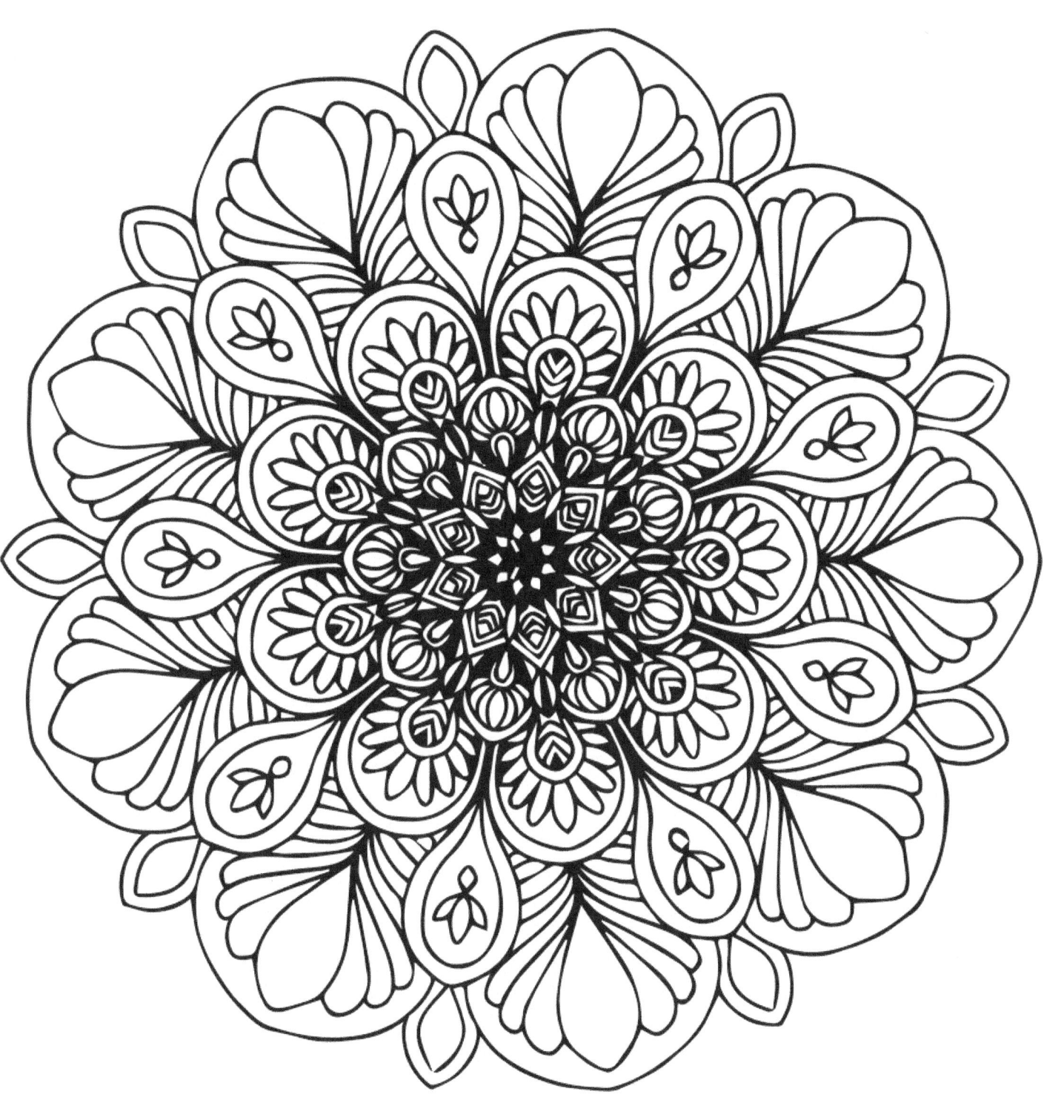

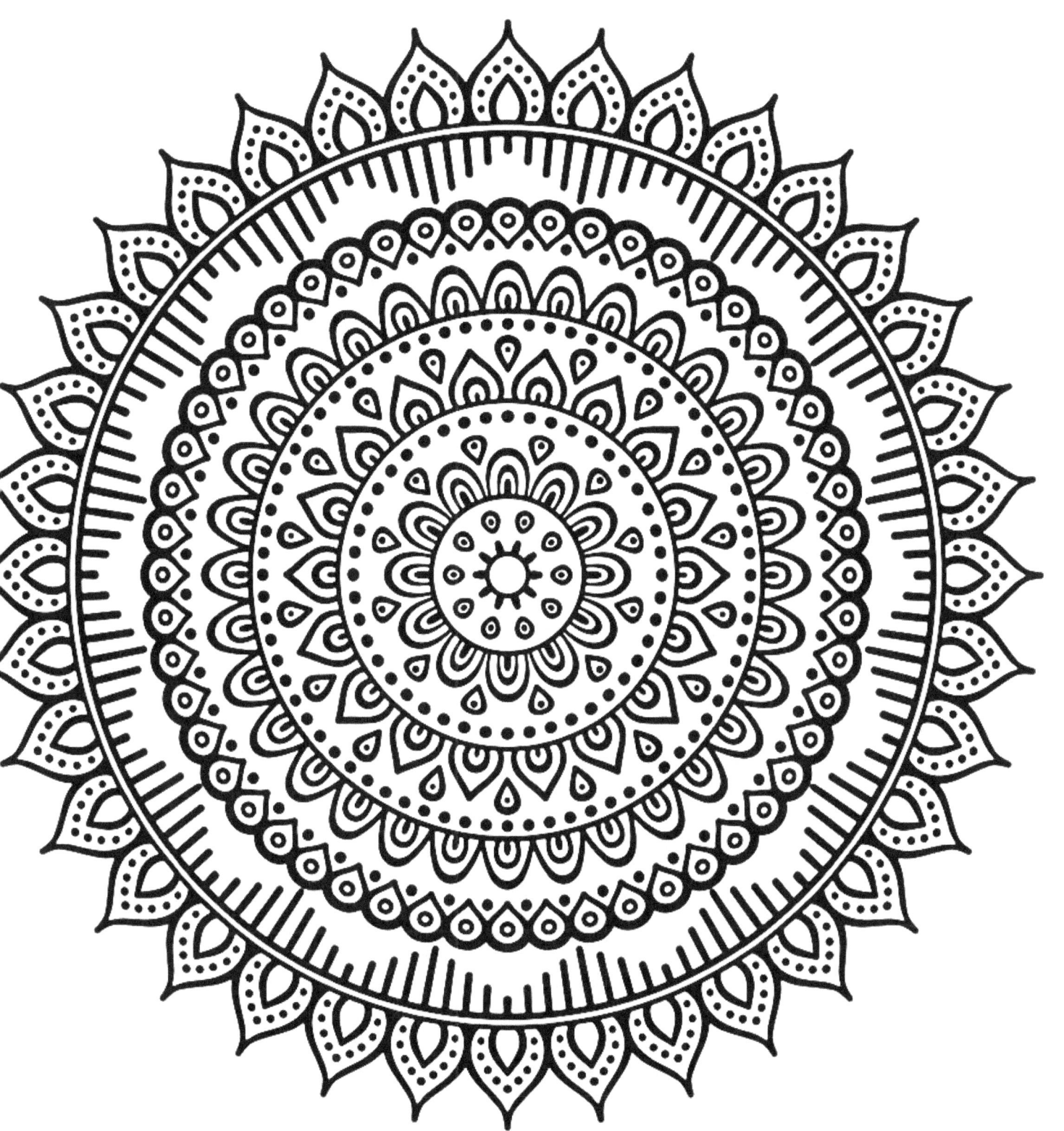

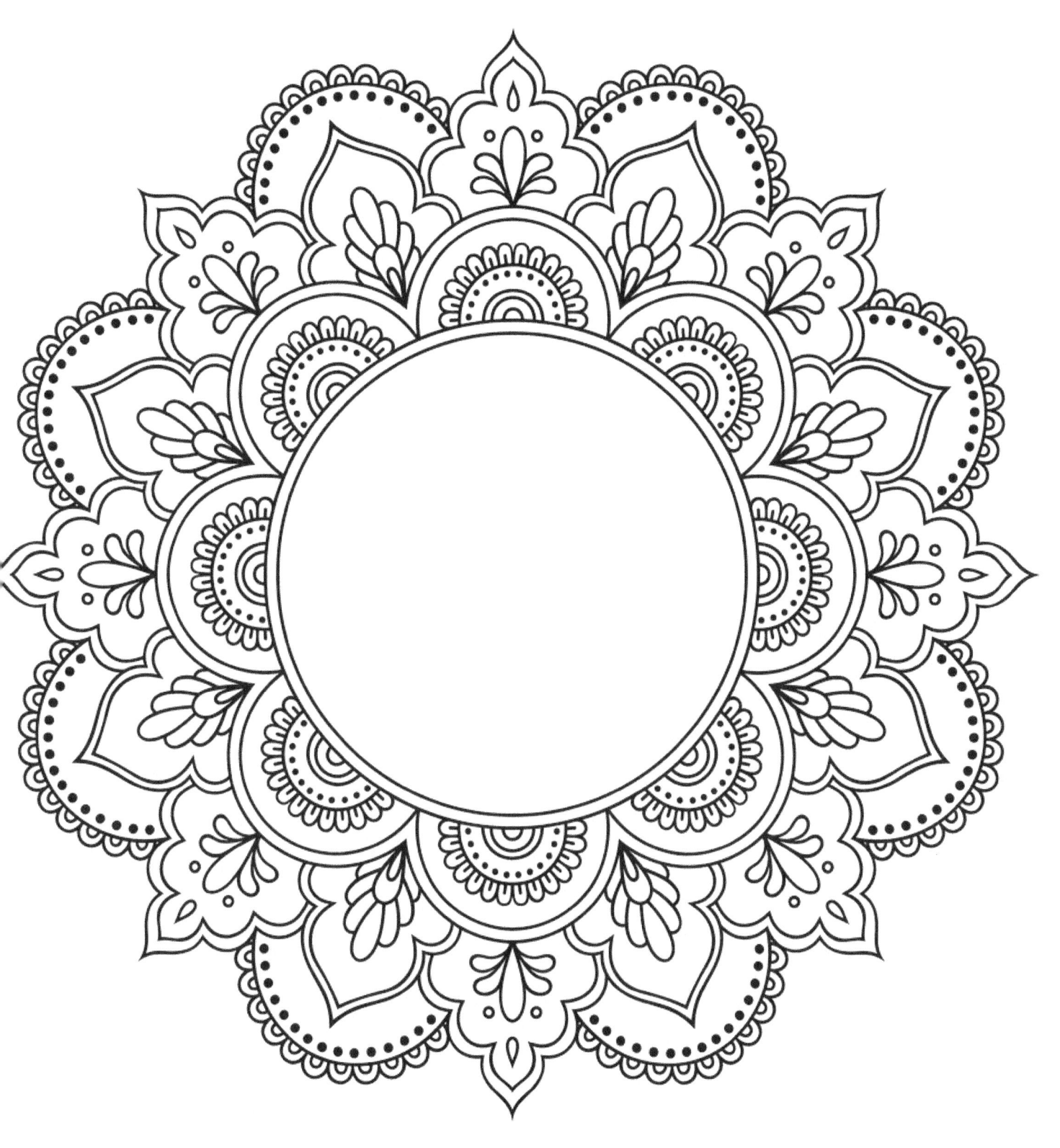

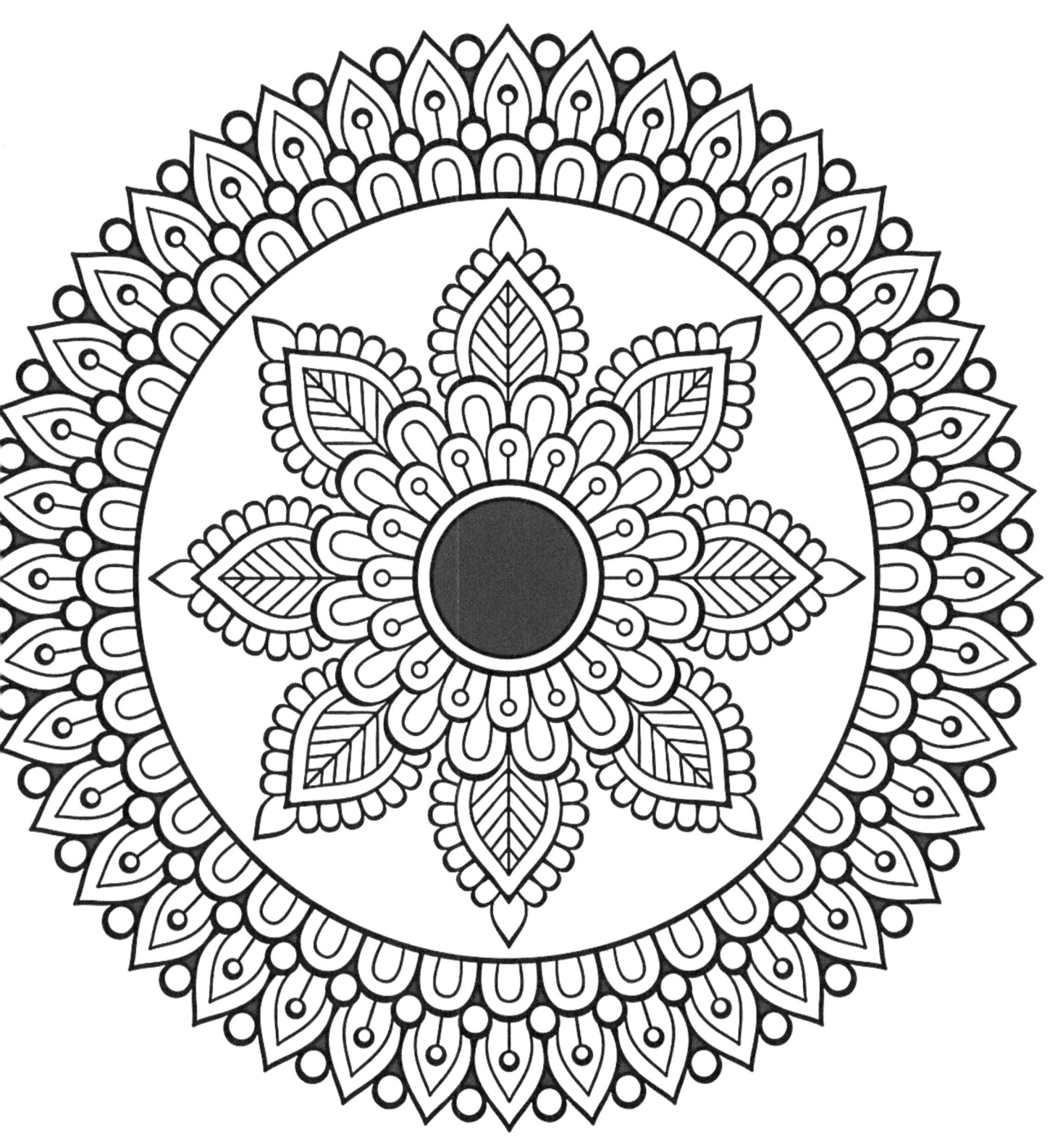

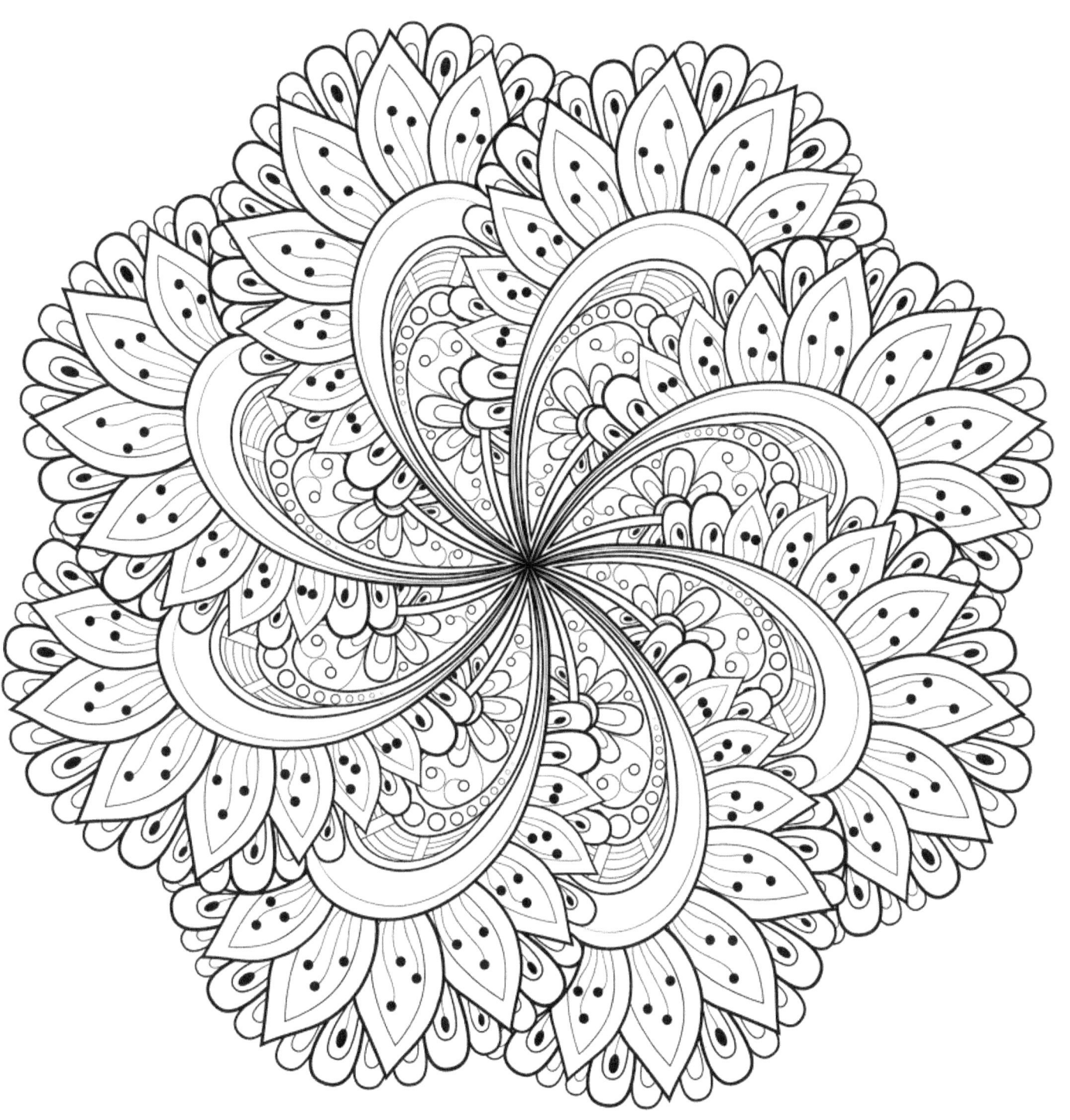

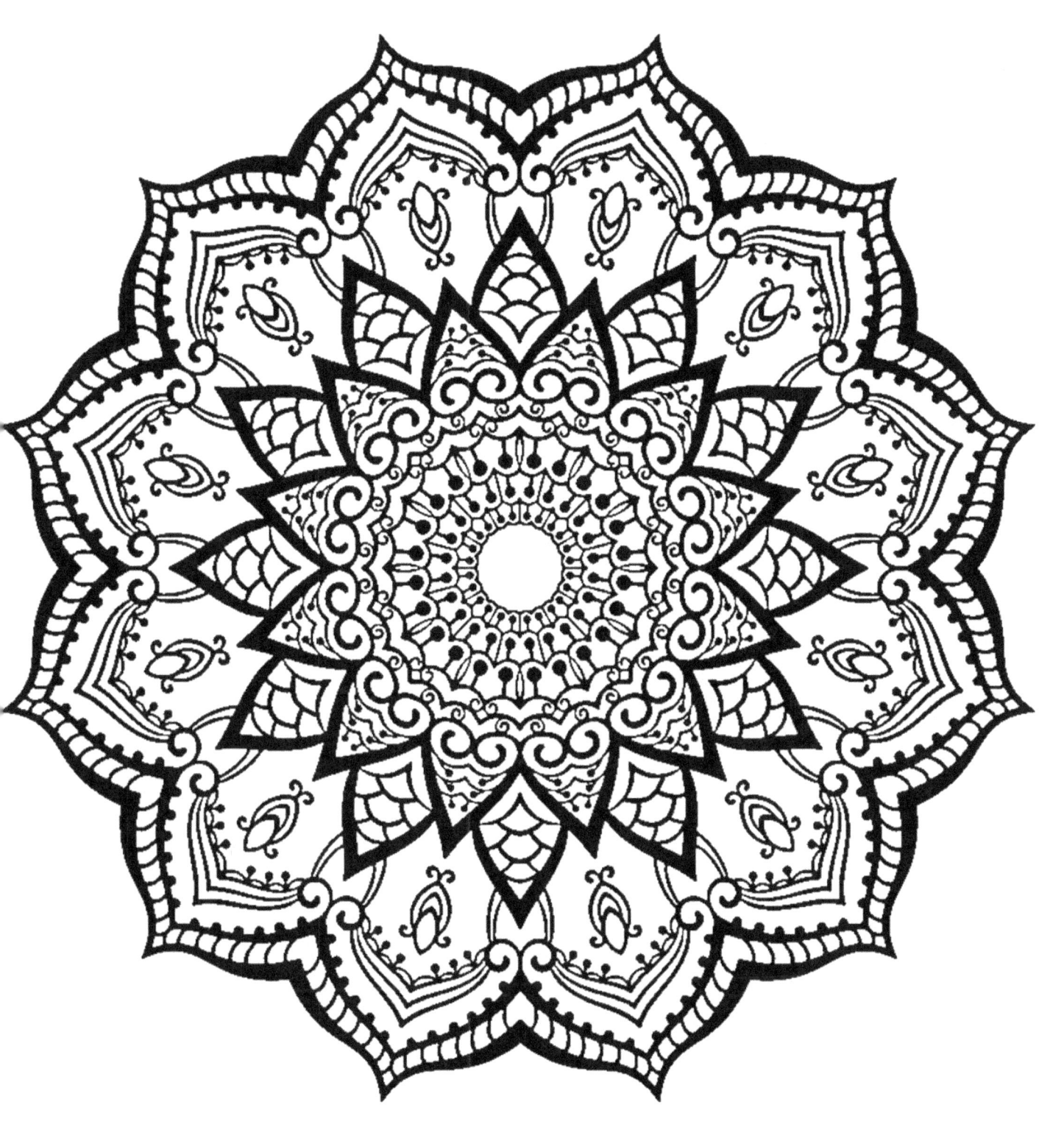

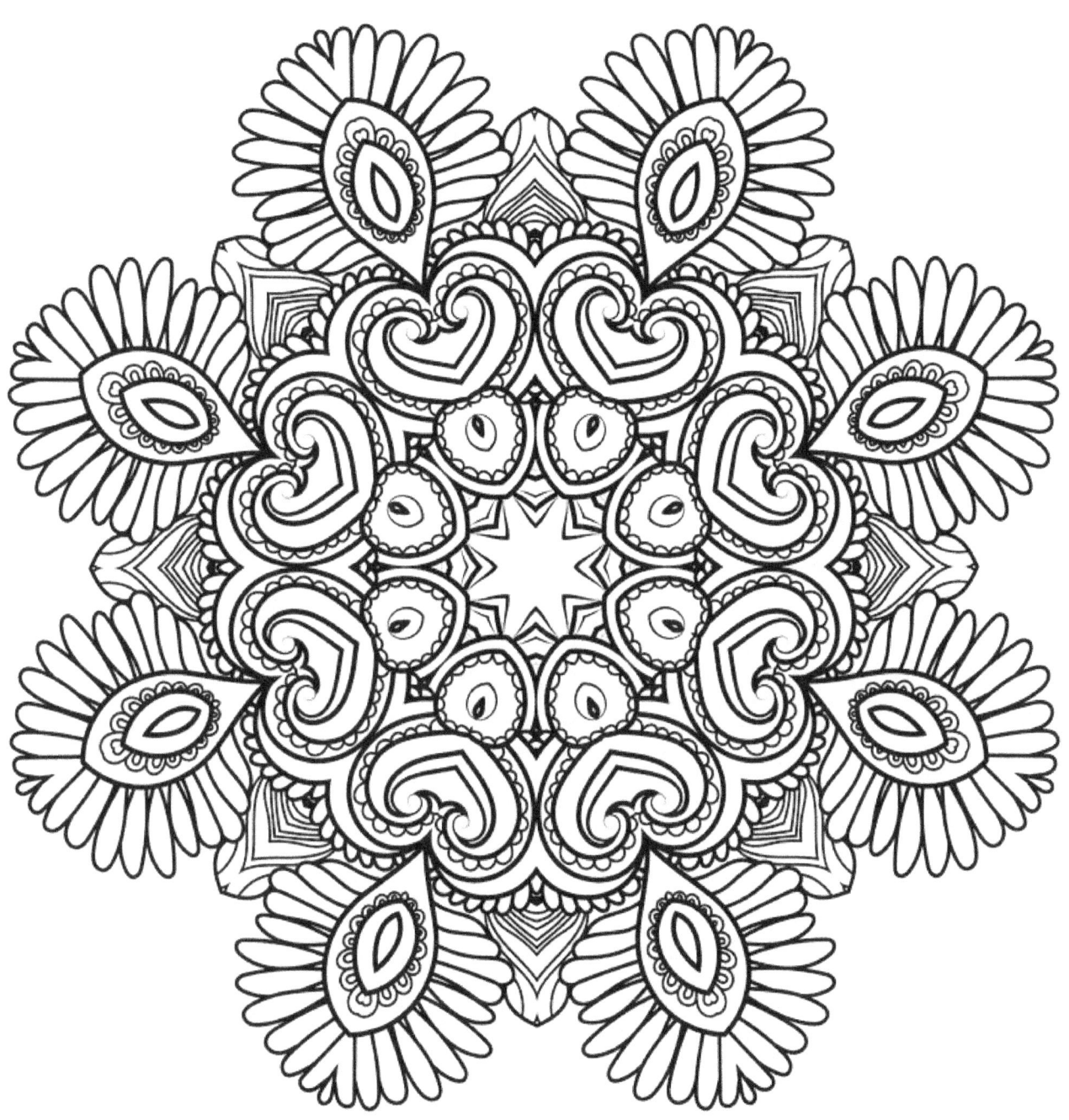

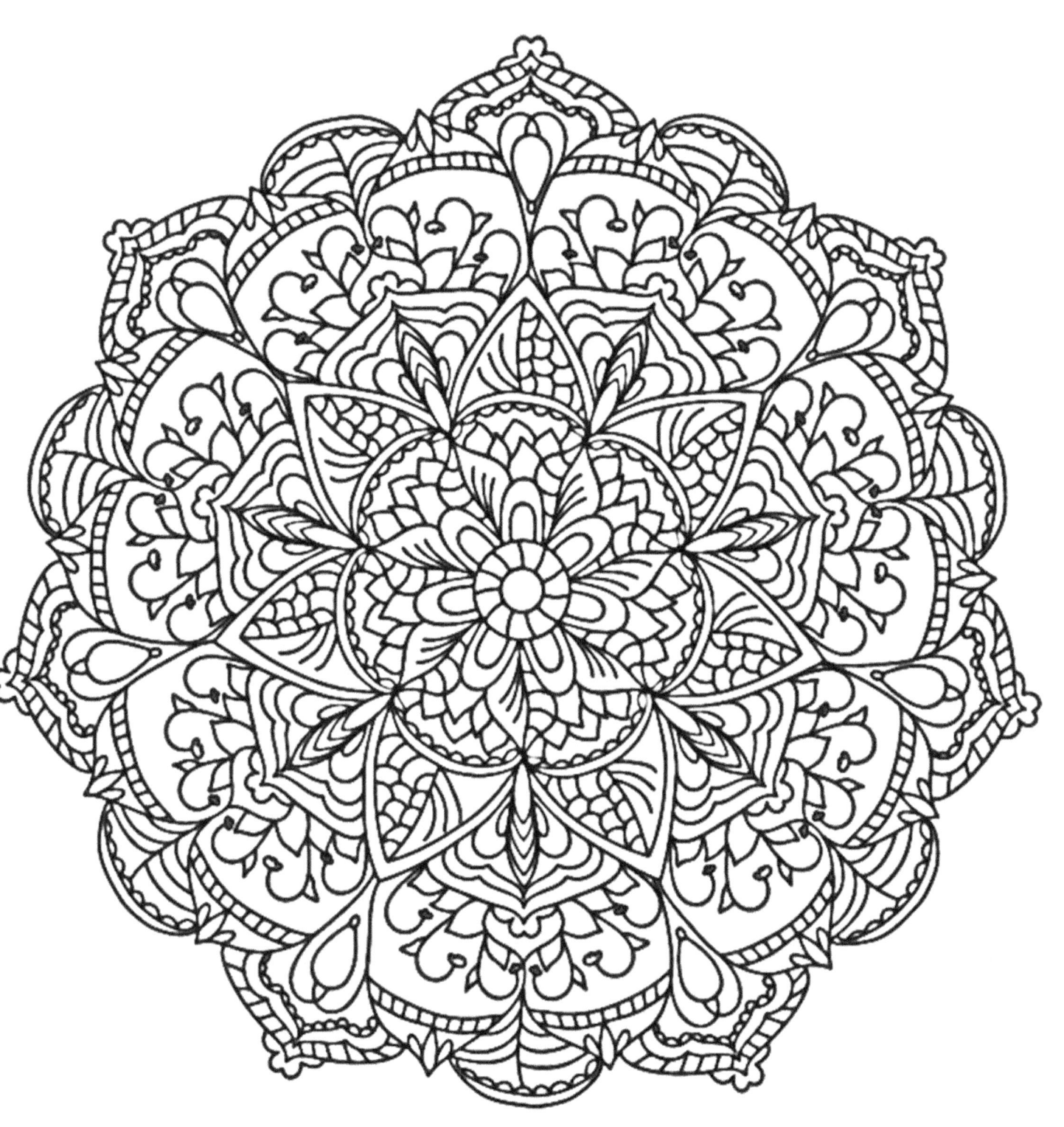

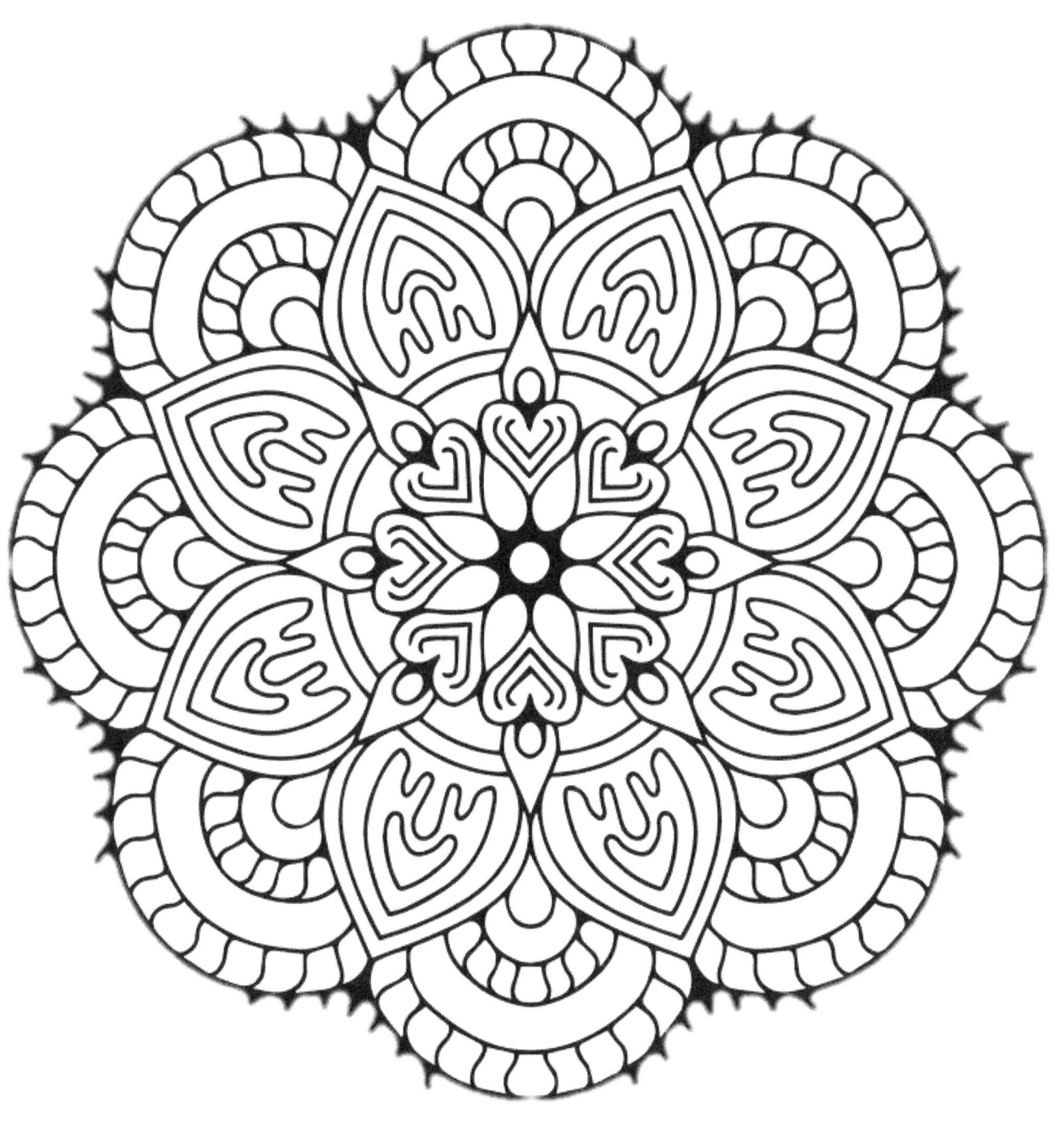

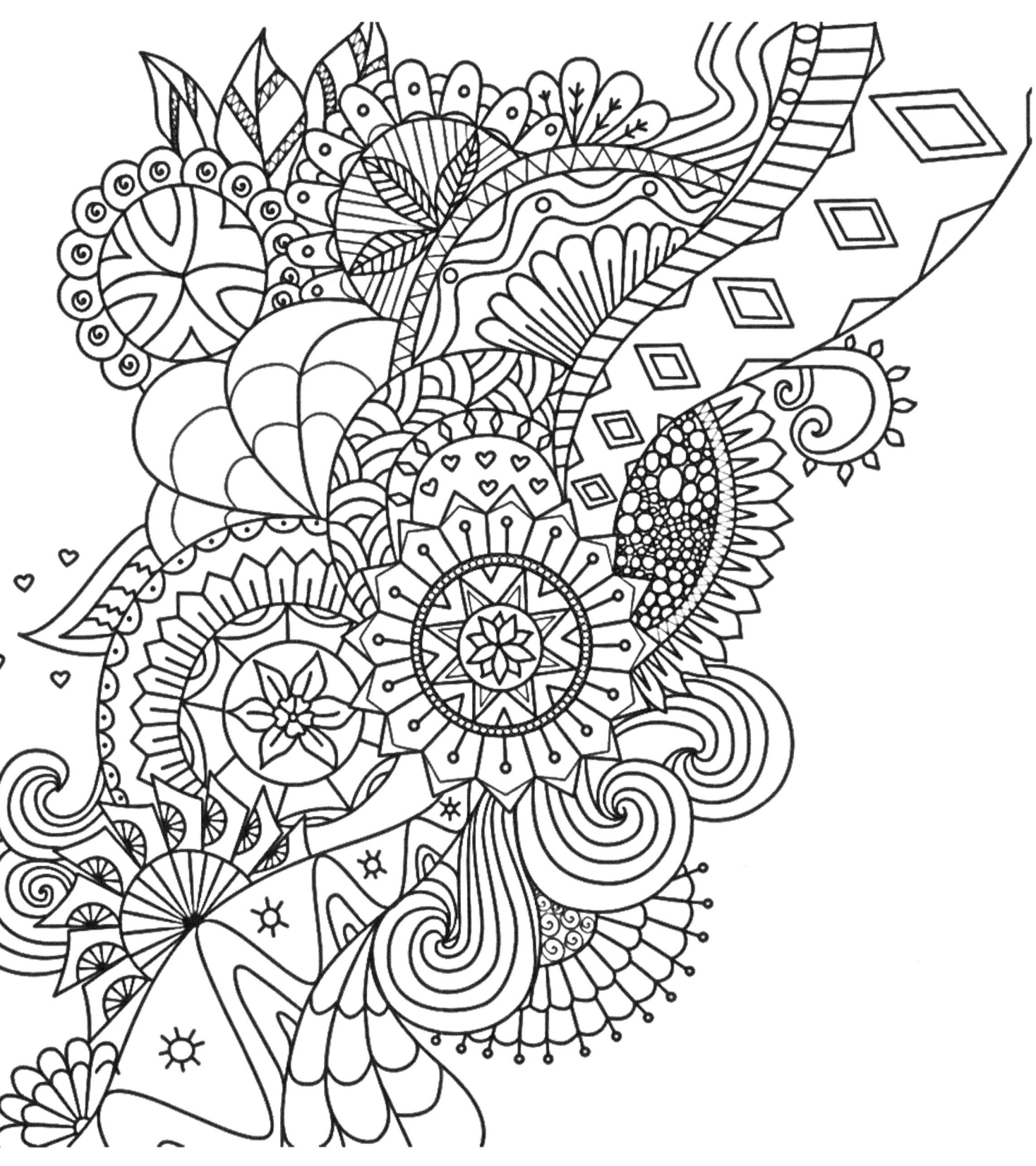

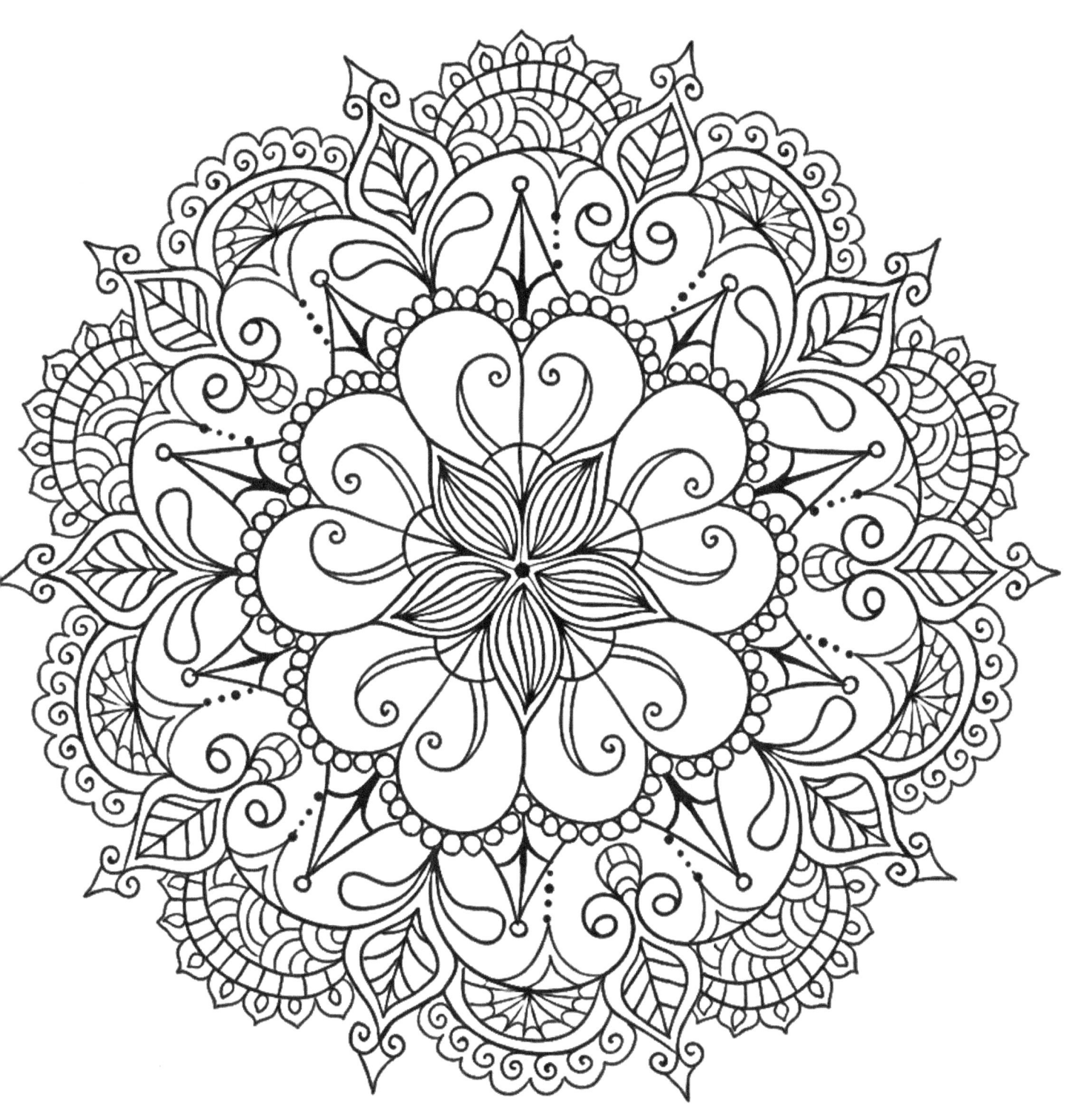

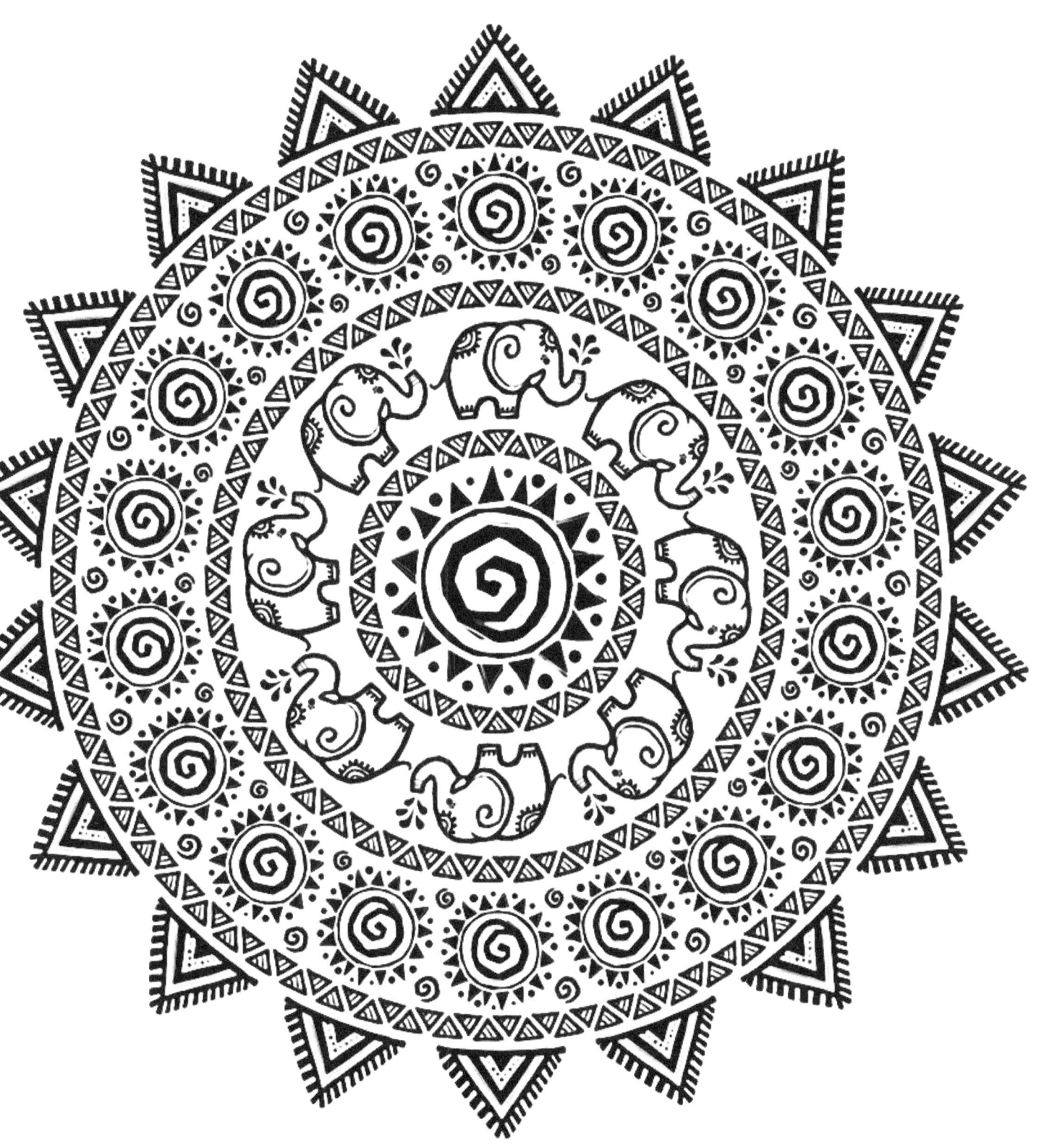

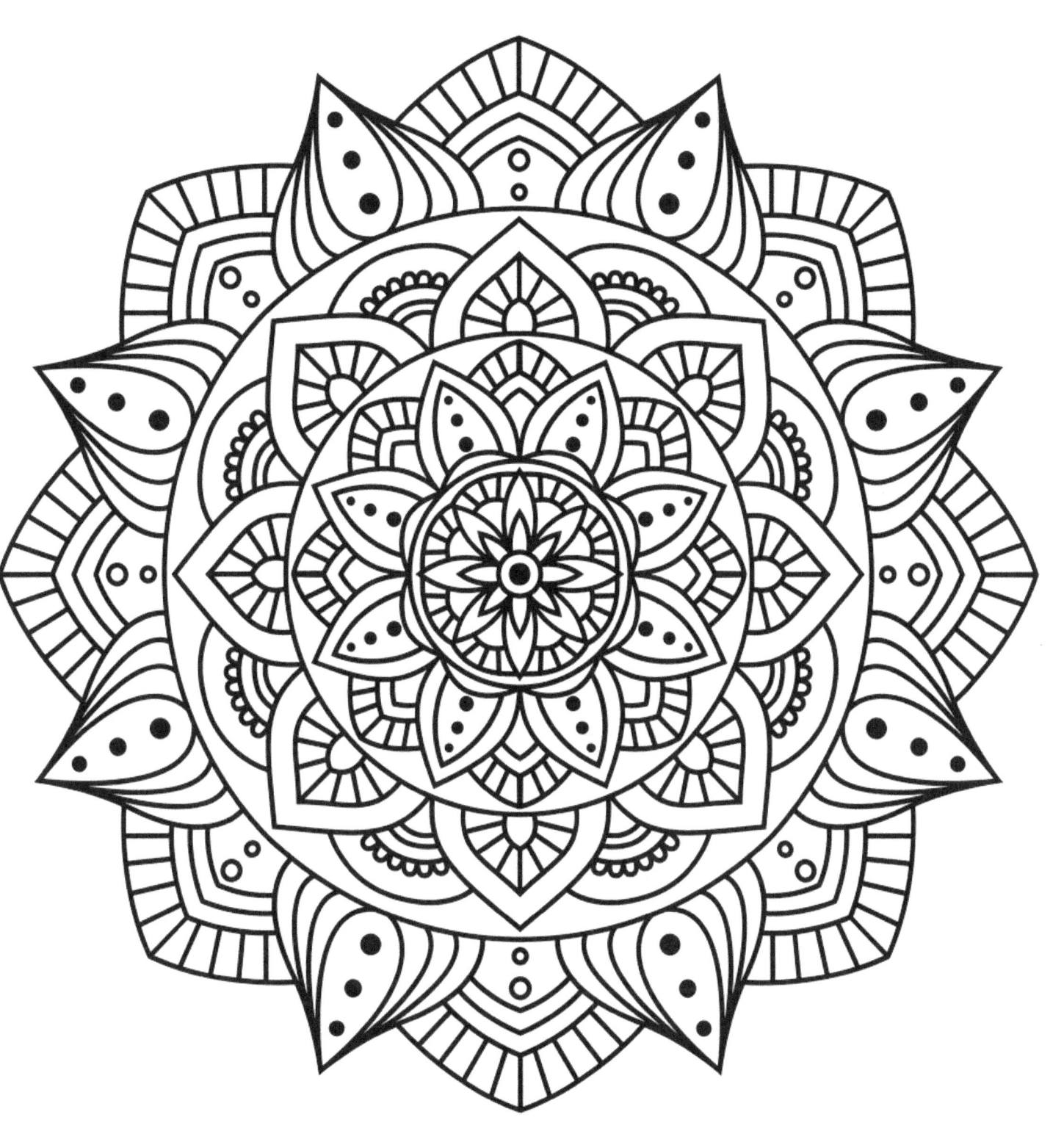

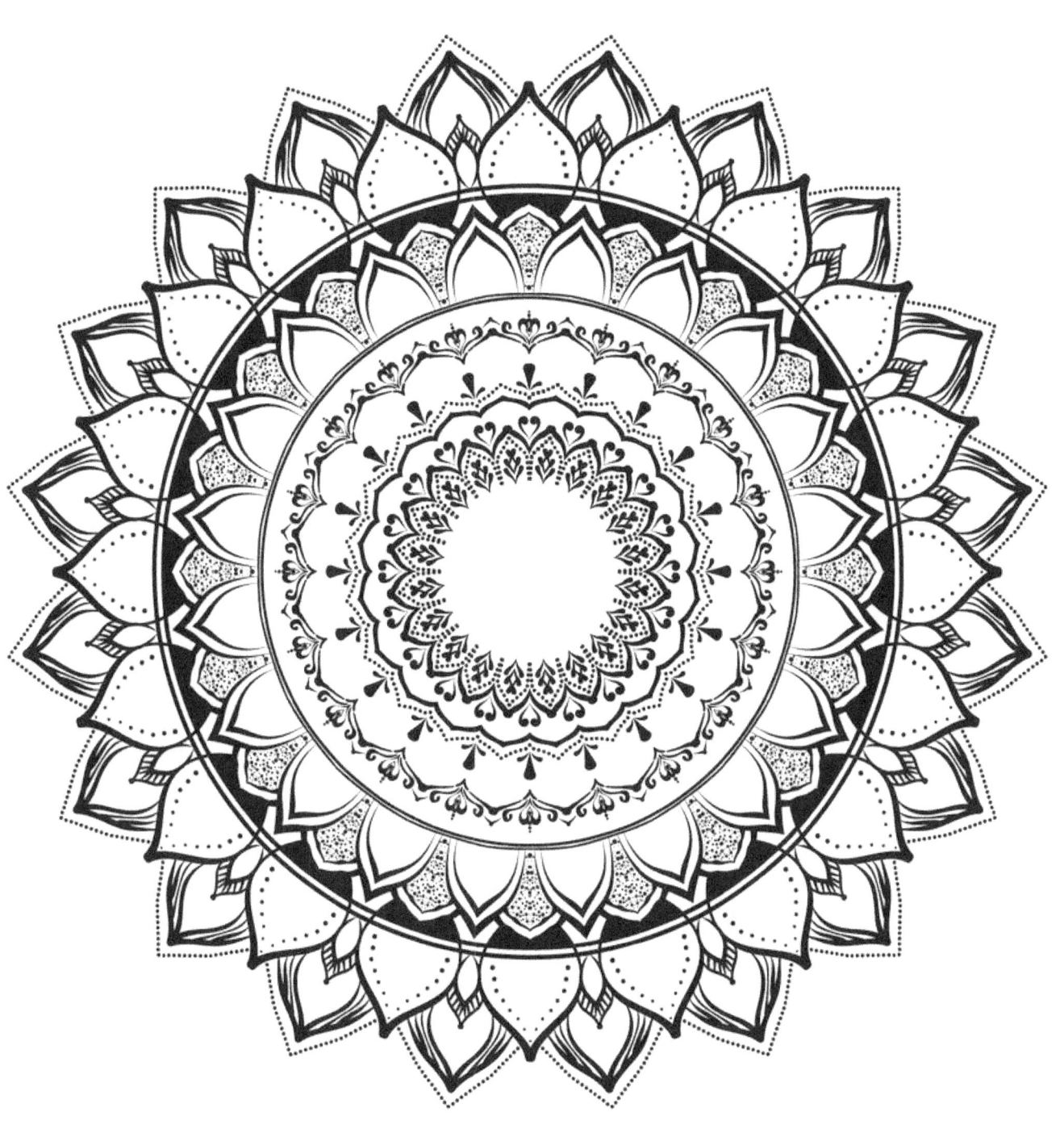

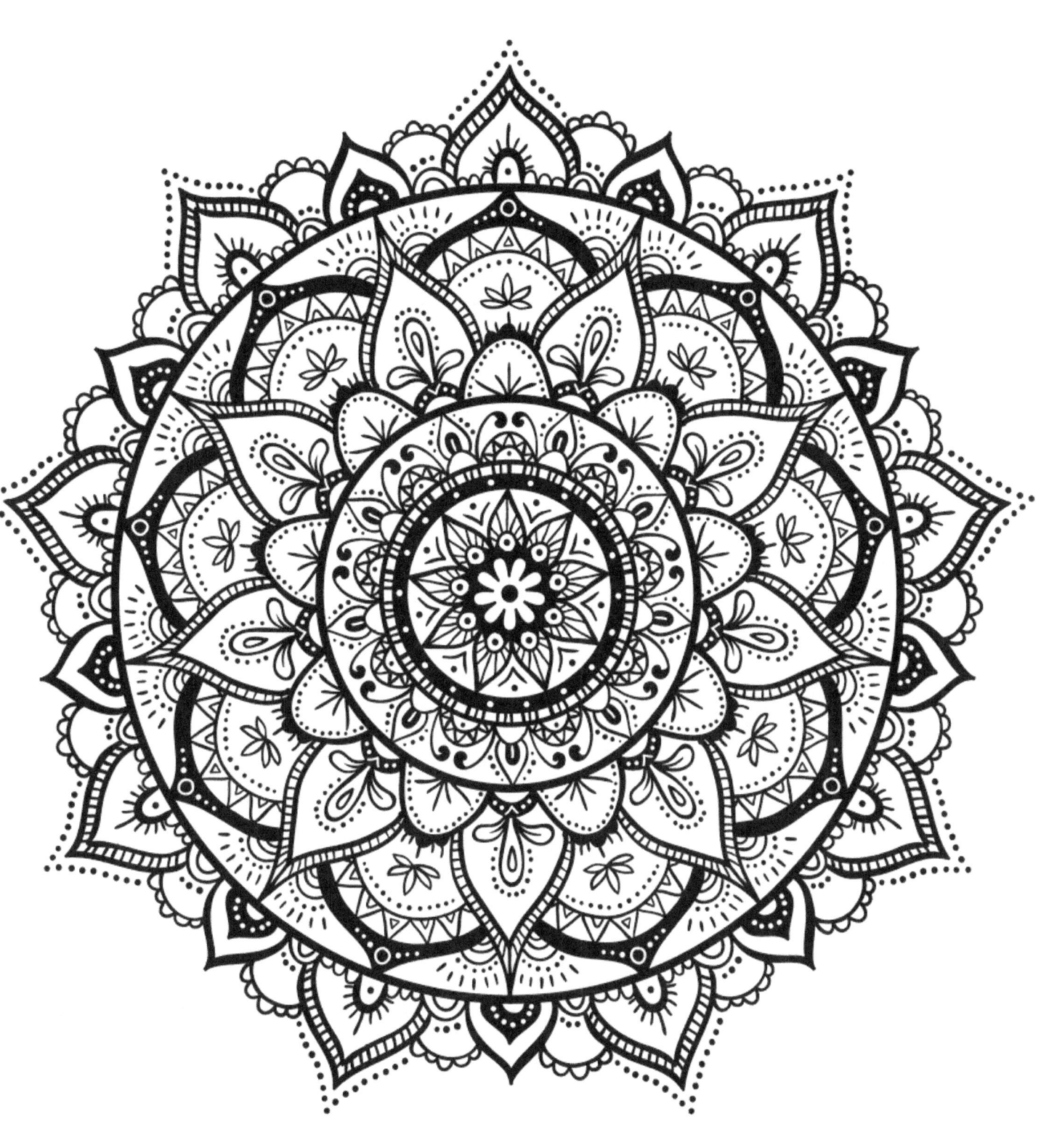

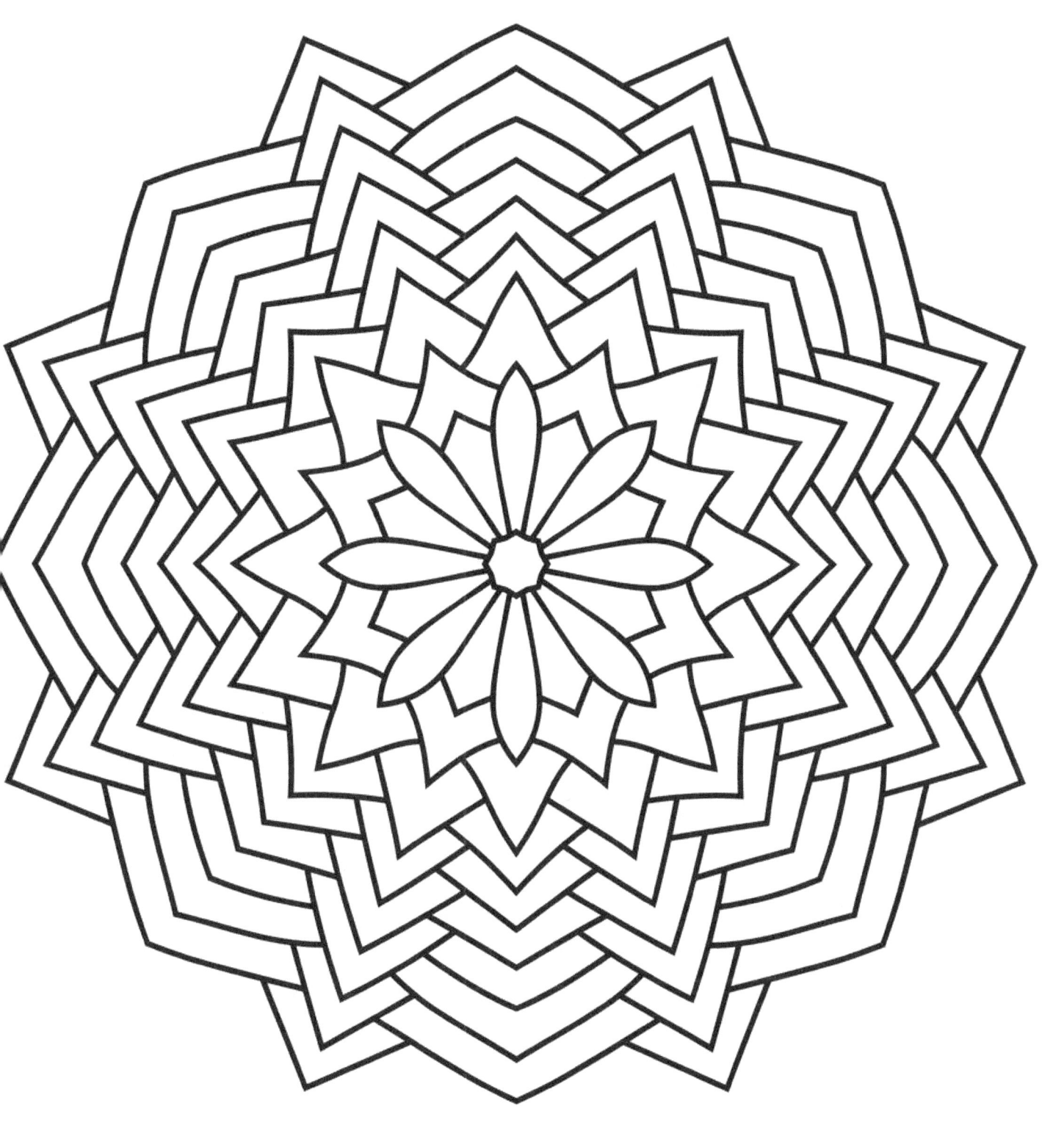

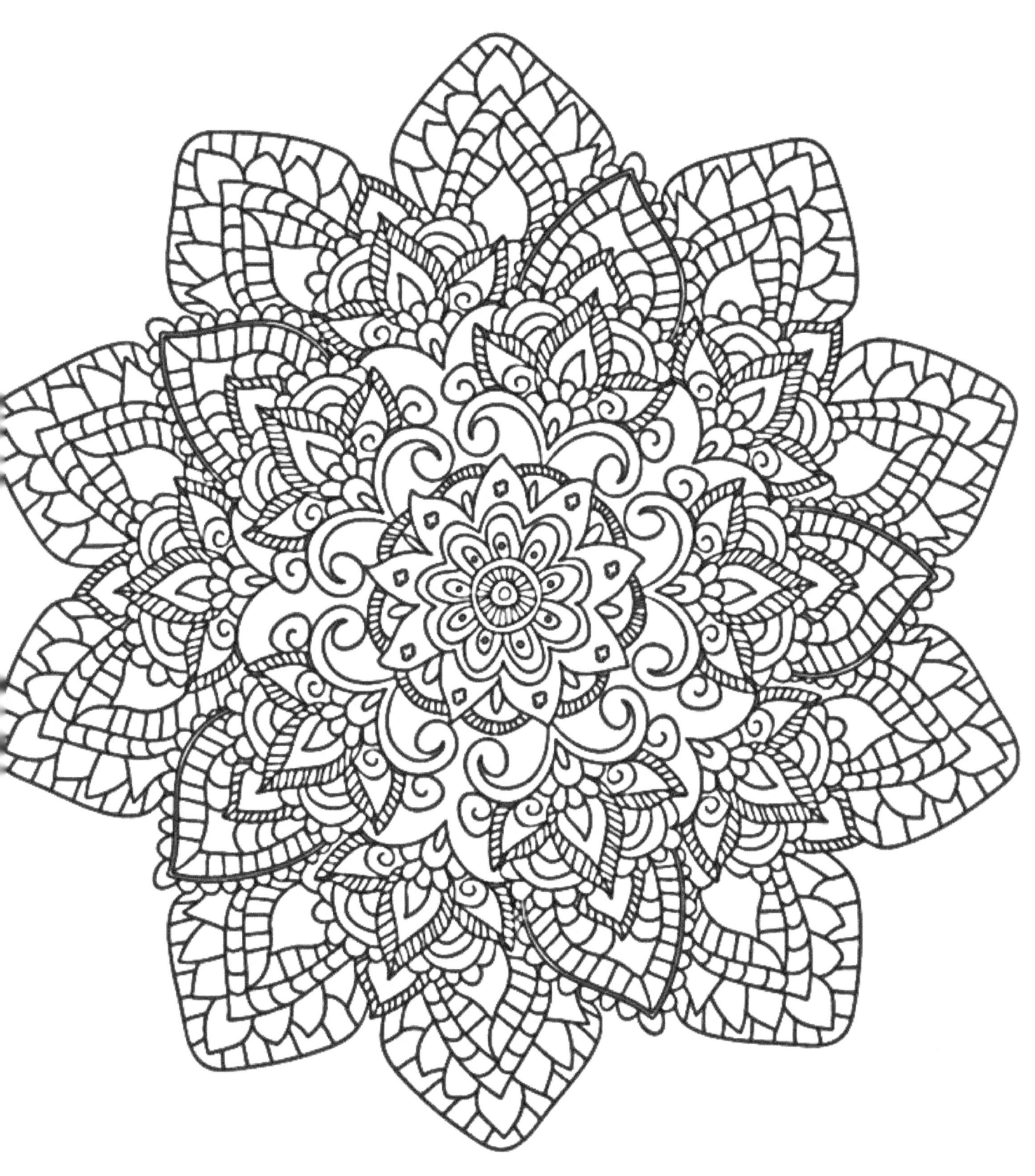

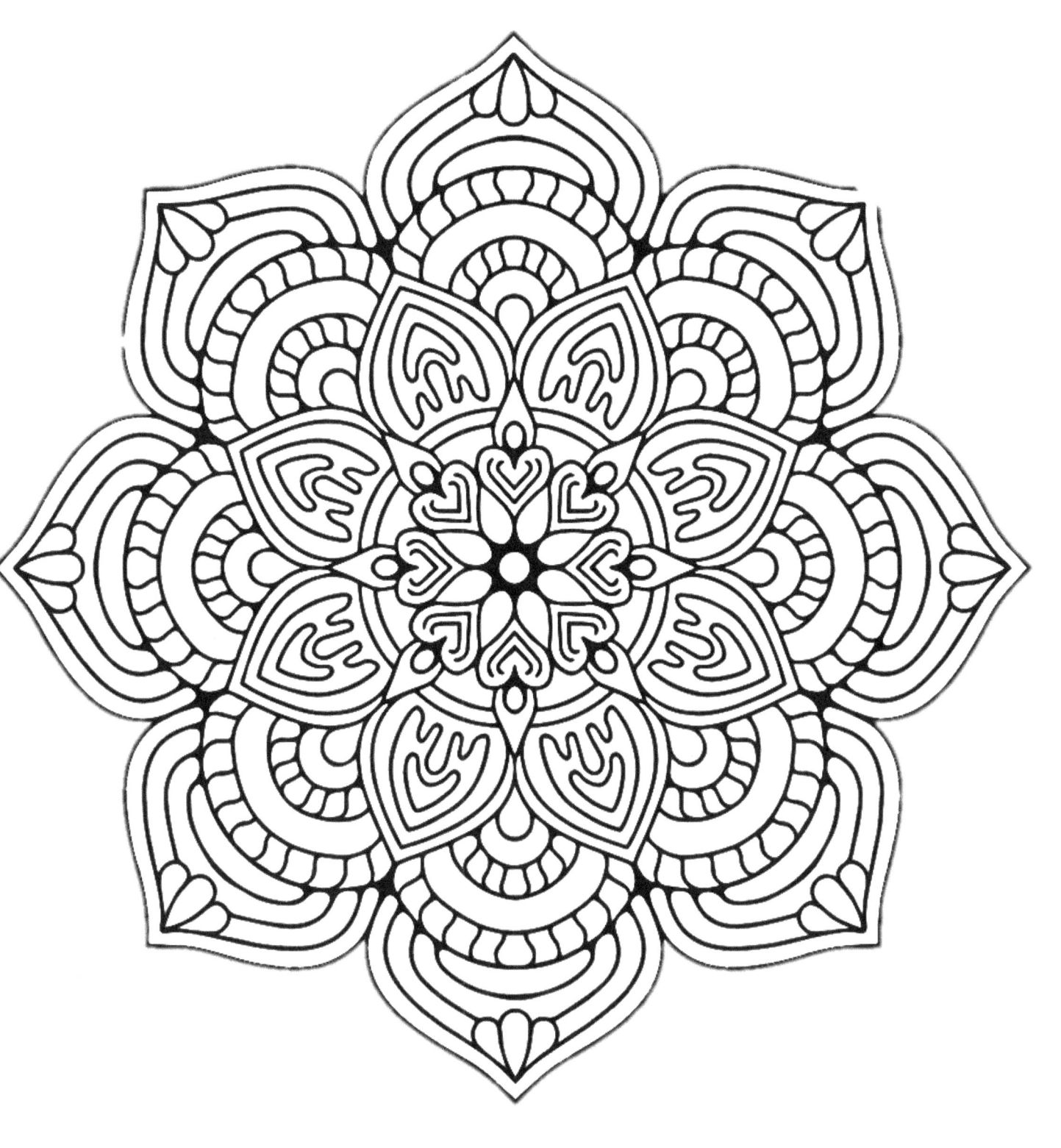

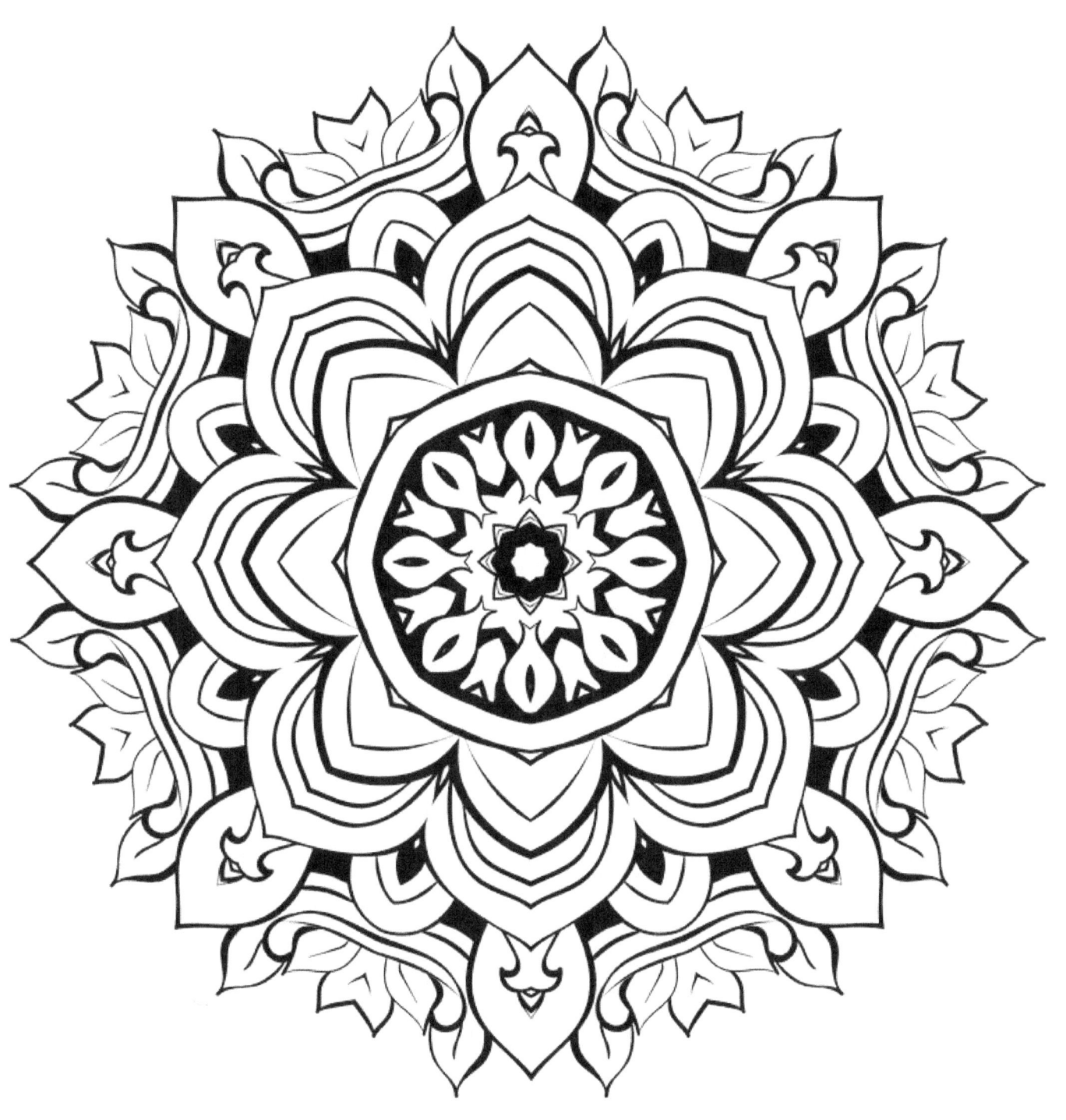

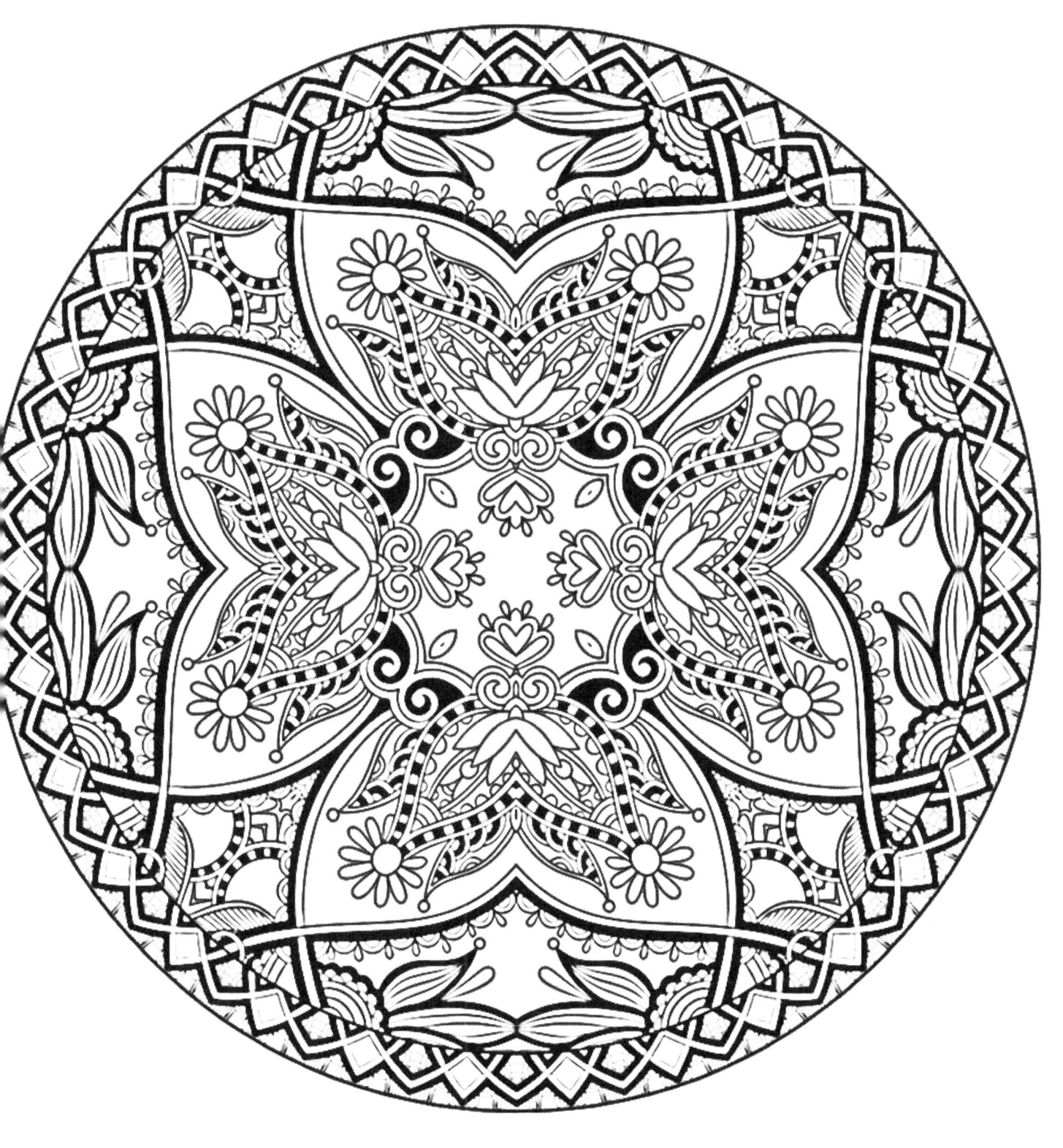

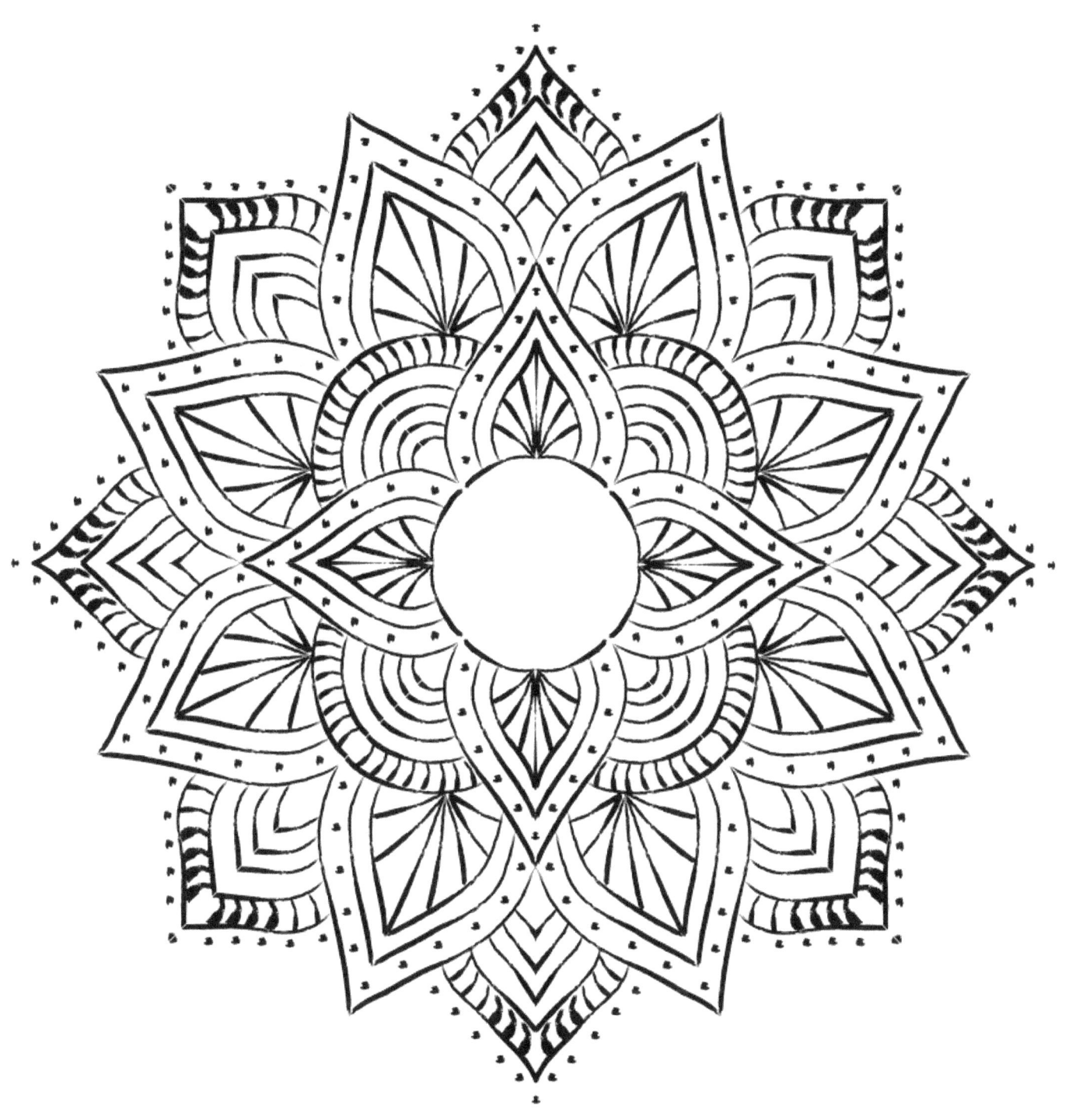

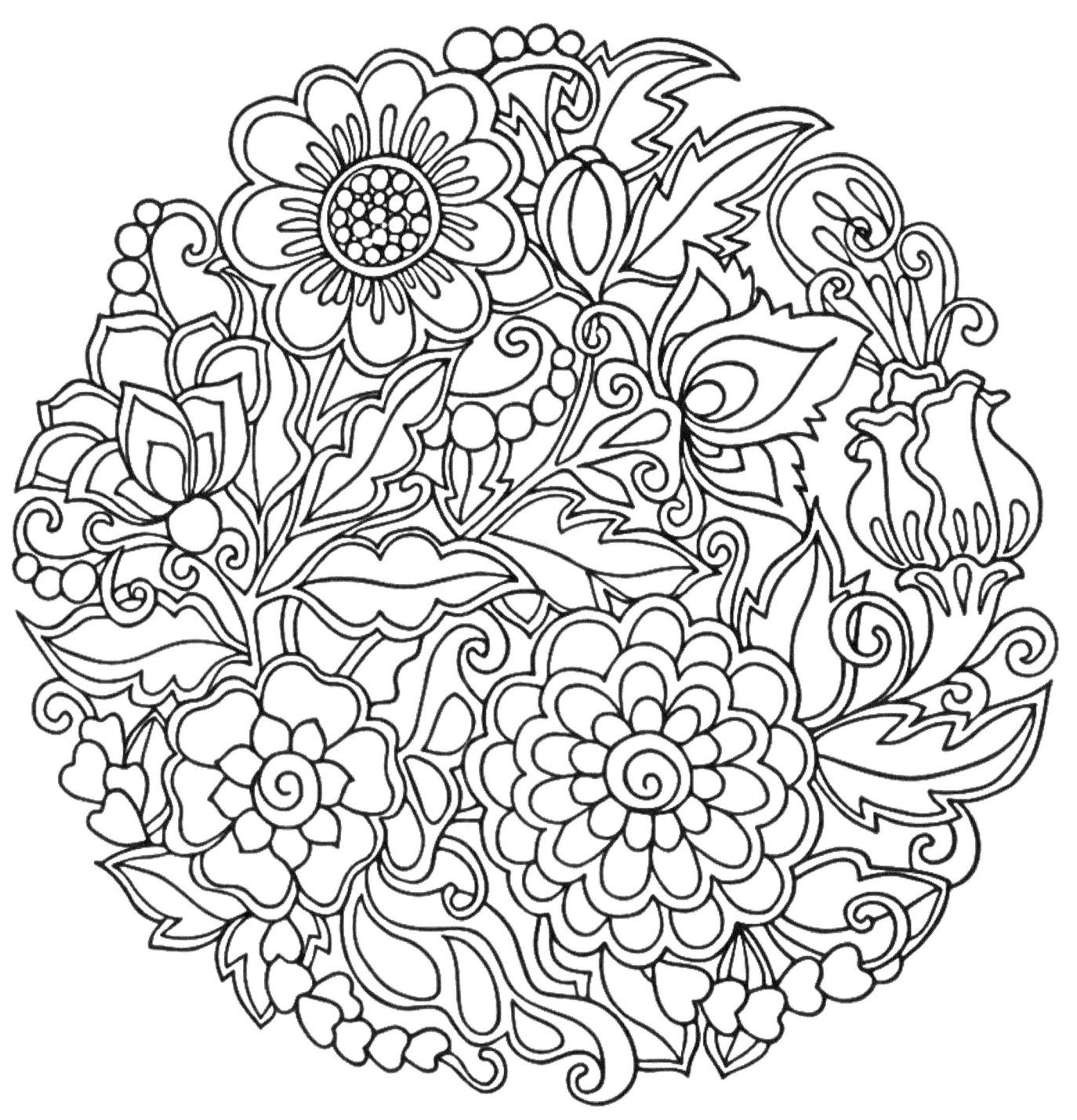

50

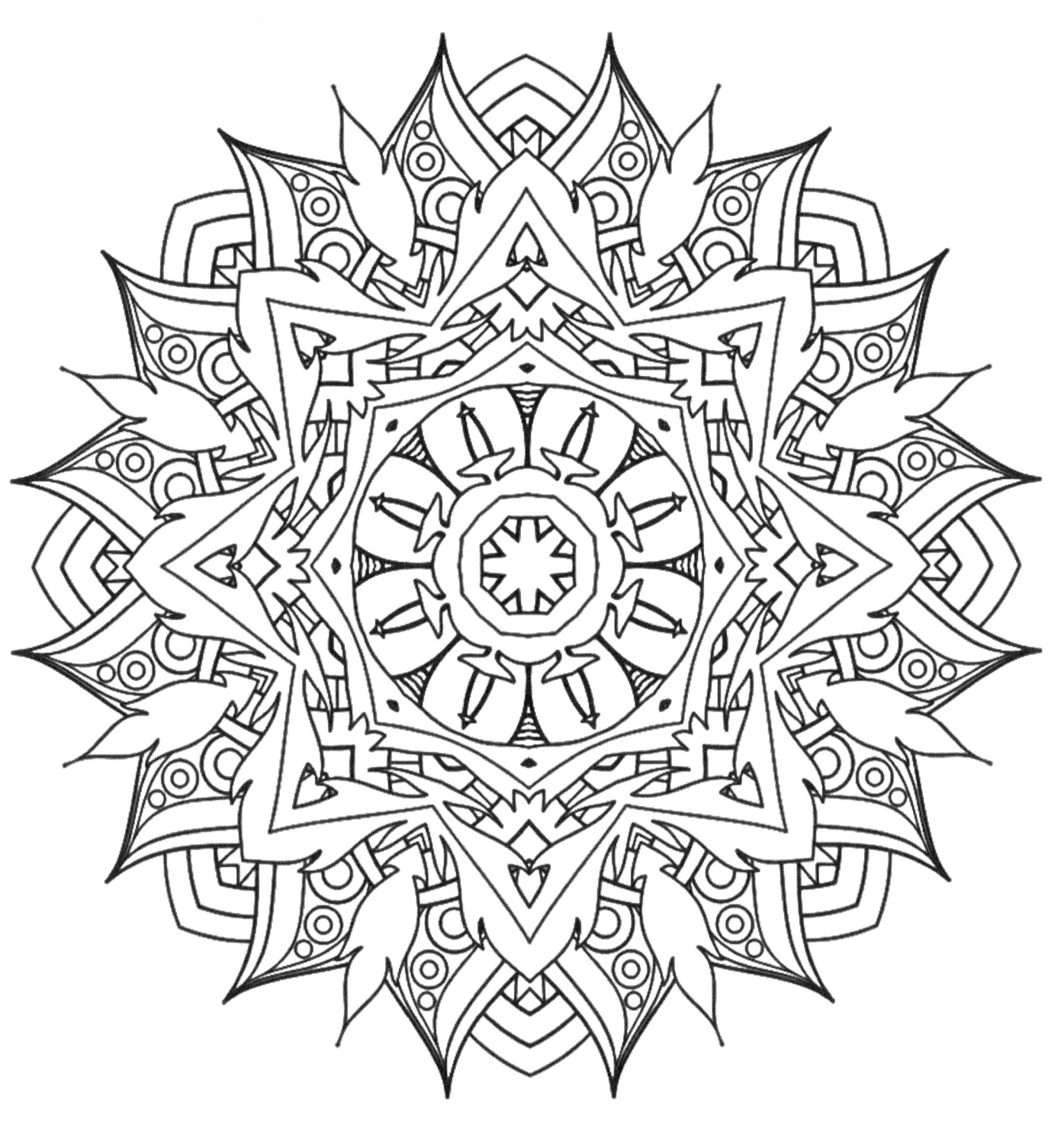

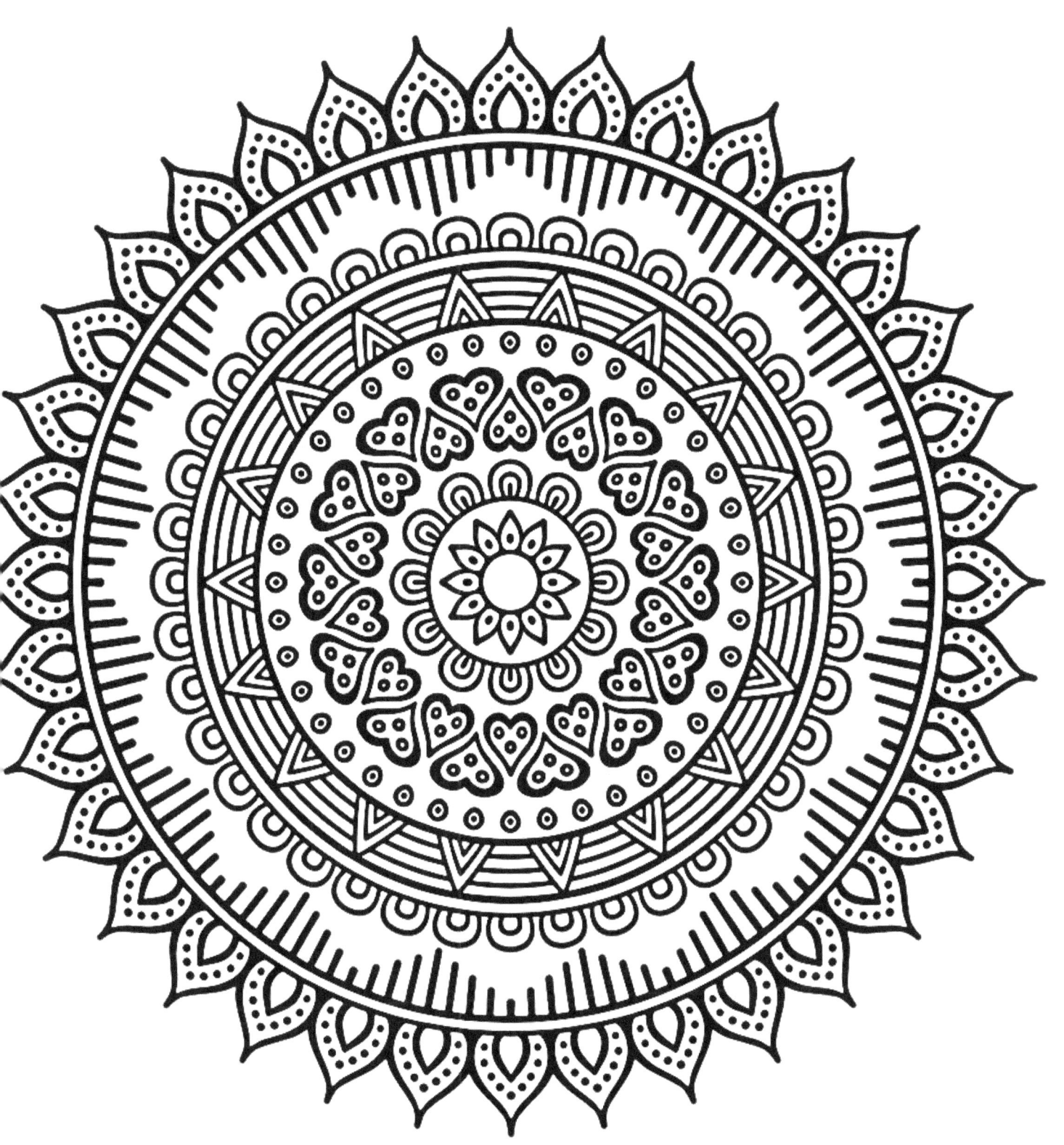

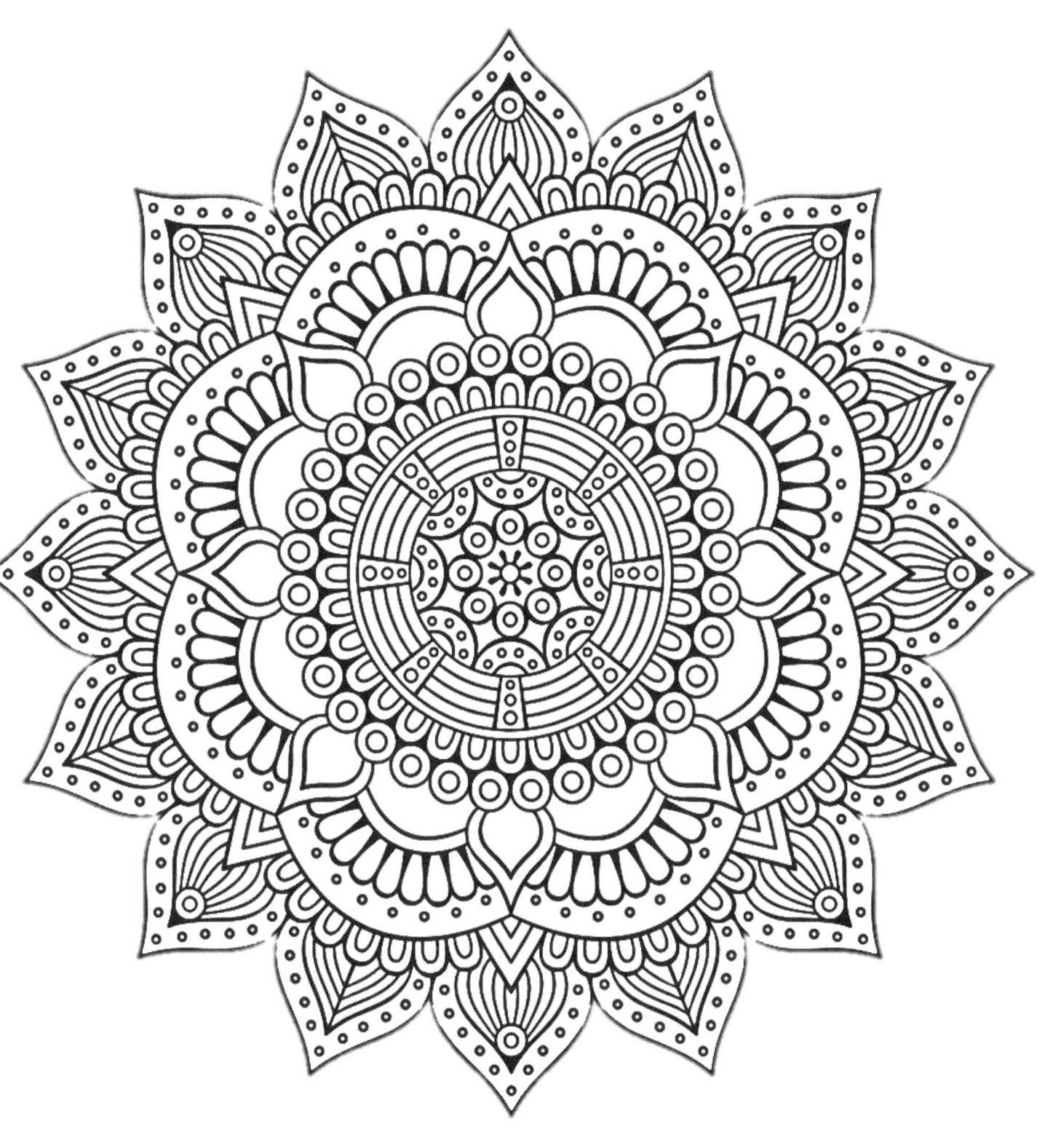

56

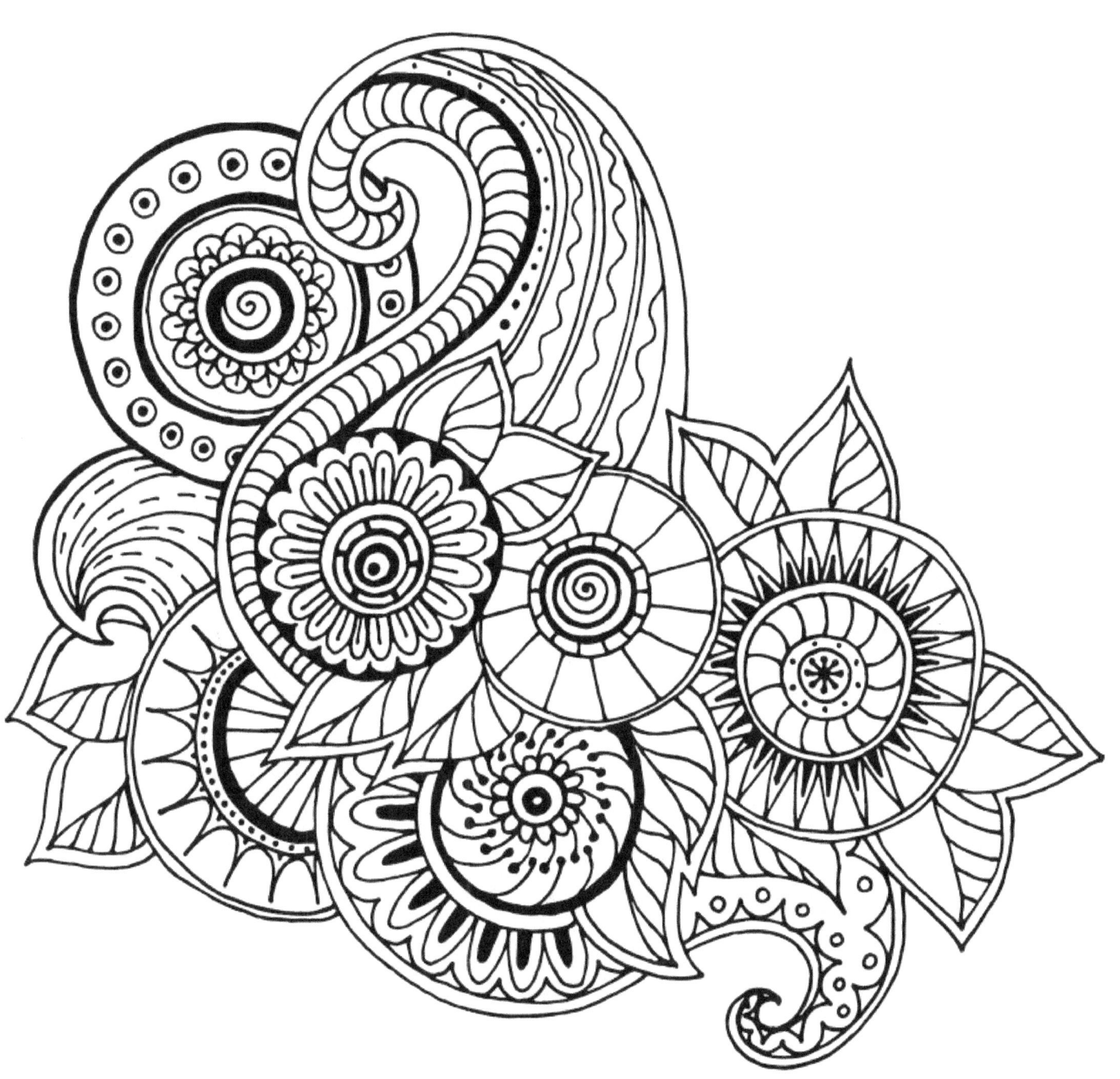

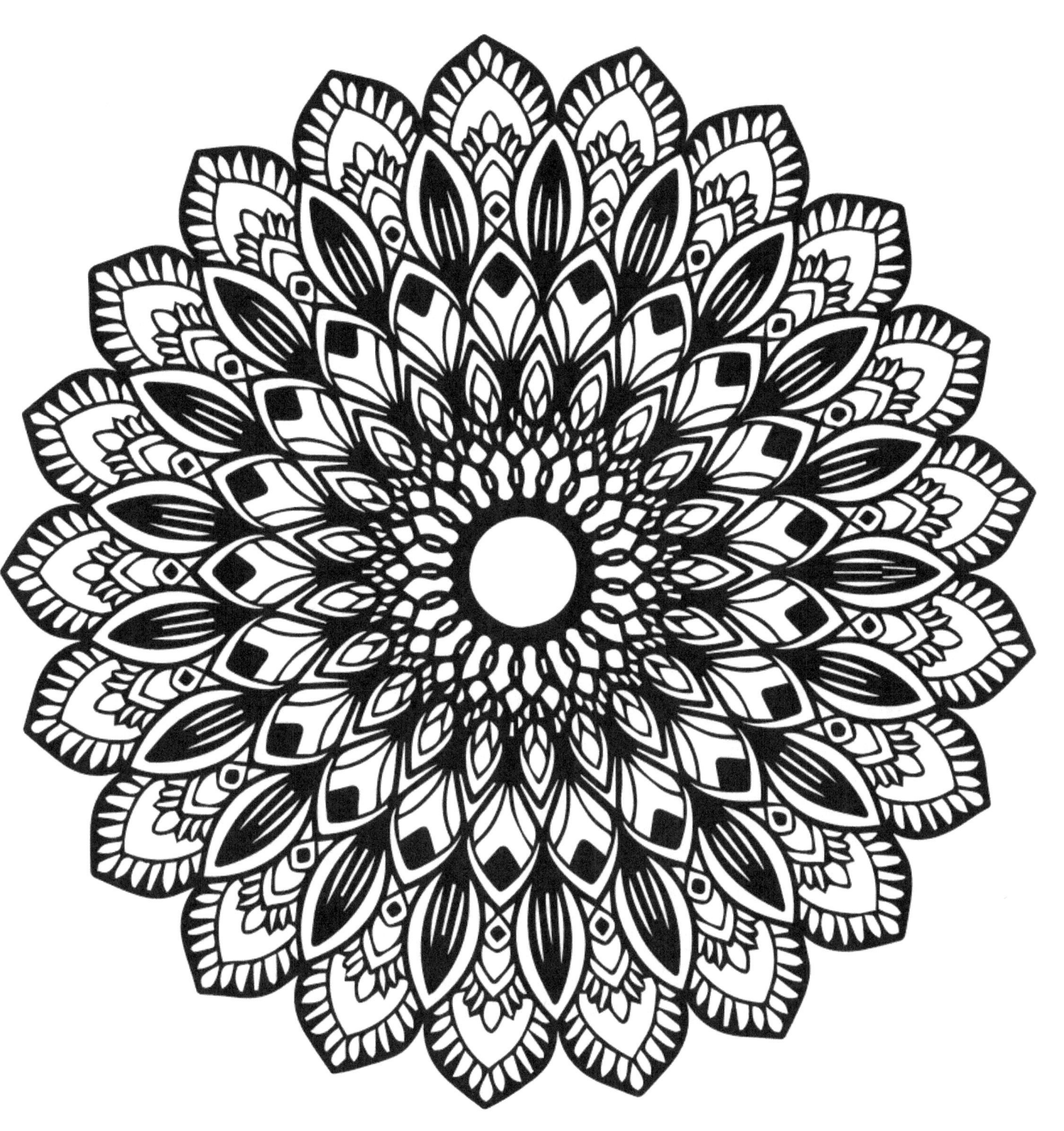

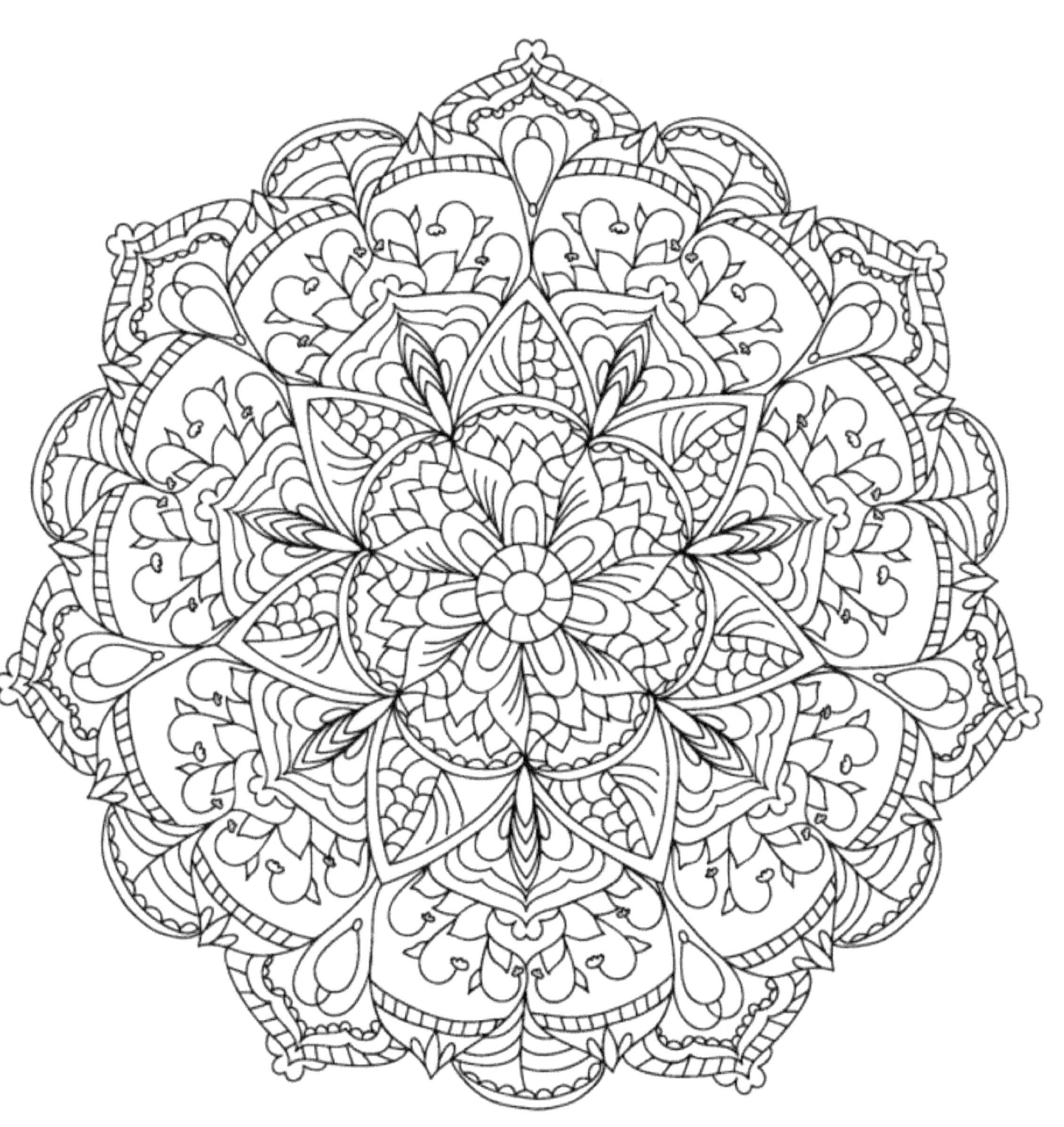

www.ingramcontent.com/pod-product-compliance
Lightning Source LLC
Chambersburg PA
CBHW082119220526
45472CB00009B/2240